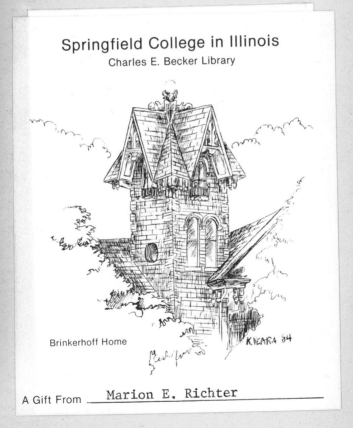

Religion and the
People of Western Europe
1789–1970

Hugh McLeod

Religion and the People of Western Europe 1789–1970

Oxford New York Toronto Melbourne

OXFORD UNIVERSITY PRESS

1981

Oxford University Press, Walton Street, Oxford OX2 6DP

London Glasgow New York Toronto
Delhi Bombay Calcutta Madras Karachi
Kuala Lumpur Singapore Hong Kong Tokyo
Nairobi Dar es Salaam Cape Town
Melbourne Auckland

and associate companies in
Beirut Berlin Ibadan Mexico City

First published as an Oxford University Press paperback and
simultaneously in a hardback edition 1981

British Library Cataloguing in Publication Data

McLeod, Hugh
Religion and the people of Western Europe
1789-1970. - (OPUS)
1. Europe - Religion
I. Title
200'.94   BR738.2
ISBN 0-19-289101-4
ISBN 0-19-215832-5 Pbk

Printed in Great Britain by
Richard Clay (The Chaucer Press) Ltd.
Bungay, Suffolk

Preface

This book starts from the assumption that the period from the French Revolution to the 1960s forms a distinct phase in western Europe's religious history. The central theme of the period was a widespread revolt against the various official churches that had emerged triumphant from the turmoil of the Reformation and Counter-Reformation, and the consequent breakdown of the religious unity that had been imposed in most areas. In Calvinist Holland a large Catholic minority had survived, and in Ireland the great majority remained Catholic, in spite of the efforts of their English rulers; also, in England, Scotland and Holland, substantial groups of dissenting Protestants were able to establish themselves. But in the later eighteenth century the Iberian Peninsula was homogeneously Catholic, the Scandinavian countries were homogeneously Lutheran; many parts of Germany were overwhelmingly of one religion, and in France the Protestant minority had been reduced to very small proportions. Even in those countries which allowed some degree of religious freedom, dissenters suffered numerous disabilities, and the lives of the great majority were closely bound up with the official churches.

From 1789 on, the attack on the power and influence of the official churches was an integral part of any attack on the existing political and social order, and the demand for religious freedom and equality became an essential part of any programme of liberal reform. In these years religion became a fundamental source of division in west European societies, and nearly all of them saw the formation of organised blocs of believers and unbelievers, clericals and anti-clericals, state church supporters and sectarians. This is why the nineteenth century was both the archetypal period of secularisation, and a great age of religious revival: as large numbers were alienated from the official church, religion ceased to provide a focus of social unity; but it became instead a major basis for the distinctive identity of specific communities, classes, factions in a divided society. Many people found their loyalty to their churches intensified in the process.

Chapters 1 and 2 trace the various patterns of religious polarisation that were established in the earlier part of this period: Chapter 1 shows how religion became integral to the conflict between Right and Left during the revolutionary years in France, and remained so in most parts of western Europe throughout the nineteenth century, and well into the twentieth; Chapter 2 shows how economic change widened the gulf between the religious life of rich and poor, and perhaps of men and women. Chapter 3 looks at the kinds of religious movements that flourished most vigorously in these conditions, and at the widespread tendency in the later nineteenth century for ideological communities with fundamentally opposed views of the world to build their own ghettos. Chapters 4-7 look at the characteristic forms of religion in town and countryside, in the working class and in the urban middle class, and at the consequences for religion of the mass movement of population from country to city. Chapter 8 looks at the fading away of the religious patterns established in the period following the French Revolution. In some areas, notably Britain and Scandinavia, this was already happening in the early twentieth century; but in most countries these patterns remained strongly in evidence until after the Second World War, and it was the 1960s that brought this phase of religious history to an abrupt end.

Like any other book of its kind, this one is highly selective. No single author could do justice to all aspects of the religious history of western Europe during this period – even with limitless space, and a lifetime to do it in. This book concentrates heavily on England, France and Germany, and is almost entirely based on works in the English, French and German languages – though it also includes some material on Ireland, Scotland, Wales, Austria, Switzerland, the Low Countries, the Iberian Peninsula and Scandinavia. It is exclusively concerned with the gentile population of these countries: for an analysis of the effects of emancipation and urbanisation on Jewish religious life, the reader is recommended to consult Stephen Sharot's *Judaism: A Sociology*, New York, 1976. The book also highlights particular points in time, notably the 1790s, the 1880s and 1890s, and the 1960s, partly because developments in these decades seem to me especially significant, and partly because these happen to be the periods where the documentation is most abundant; on the other hand, periods like 1914–50, for which the secondary literature is much thinner, have received more superficial treatment. It is also selective in its overall approach: its main concern is with the part played by the official churches, and by other religious or anti-religious movements in the life of the various sections of the population, and with the ways in which the character and social role of religion changed as a result of the liberalisation and democratisation of society, urbanisation and the development of capitalism. I have accordingly emphasised class relationships, as these seem to me to have had a fundamental bearing on these issues, and I have paid much less attention to, for instance, developments in philosophy or religious thought, which seem to me to have had less effect in these areas. Similarly, because of my stress on the social role of churches and religious movements, there is relatively little discussion of individual religious experience. In the Further Reading section I have mentioned some of the most interesting books in the areas covered by each chapter, and named those authors whose work I have drawn particularly heavily upon. I have used the notes to identify quotations, to indicate obscure sources, or to provide some support for controversial or unexpected assertions.

I want to thank Paul Thompson and Thea Vigne for allowing me to quote from their interviews on family life and work experience before 1918, and Dr Frances Lannon for permission to refer to material from her unpublished D.Phil. thesis; David Gaunt for help with a section on Sweden; Derek Lomax for teaching me some Spanish, and for advice on reading on Spain; John Fletcher and Peter Jones for sharing their ideas and books at many points; and my wife, Jackie, for her continuing encouragement and support.

Contents

1   The Revolution

I

On October 30, 1793, the small commune of Ris-Orangis, to the south of Paris, closed the parish church, and adopted Brutus as its patron instead of St. Blaise. France had come a long way since those early months of the Revolution when, to quote Marcel Reinhard: 'It seemed that no meeting could take place without invoking heaven, that every success had to be followed by a Te Deum, that any symbol which was adopted had to be blessed. The tie was close then, no longer between "throne and altar", but between Revolution and altar.'[1] Another eleven years, and the Pope would travel to Paris for the coronation of the Emperor Napoleon, while in thousands of French parishes priests who had spent years in prison, in exile, or in hiding, were back in their churches supported by the state. History moved fast in those years: between 1789 and 1802 a pattern of assumptions was established that would decisively influence the religious history of France, and of many other countries, for a century and a half. The eighteenth century's attack on Christianity had been on mainly intellectual grounds, and the basic distinction had been between the scepticism of the educated and the faith of the masses. From the 1790s the lines of conflict became political and social. The initial aim of the bourgeois-dominated constitutional monarchy which ruled France from 1789 to 1792 was, not to destroy the church, but to remake the church in its own image. In the first year of the Revolution, the clergy lost many of their privileges: tithes were abolished, church lands were expropriated; monks and nuns were released from their vows, and only those engaged in socially useful work were given the option of carrying on; freedom of worship and equal civil rights were granted to non-Catholics. The Civil Constitution of the clergy, enacted in 1790, provided for a rationalised system of dioceses and parishes, staffed by a state-salaried clergy, elected on the same basis as civil officials by the male property-owners of their district; meanwhile, the ties of French Catholics with Rome were cut to a minimum.

The makers of the Civil Constitution naively hoped that a reformed church could be a continuing focus of national unity, and a means of inculcating loyalty to the new regime: by early 1791 it was evident that religion was actually the greatest source of *disunity* between Frenchmen. Many of the clergy were unhappy at the prospect of submitting to popular election, and even less happy about the regime of religious freedom, which meant that Protestants, Jews and freethinkers would have equal rights in these elections with pious Catholics. What drove many priests to revolt was the fact that the reform package was imposed by the Constituent Assembly as a *fait accompli*, and all attempts by bishops and clergy to make their own views heard were ignored. When the clergy were required to take an oath of loyalty to the Constitution, about half refused, and France had two opposing Catholic churches. When the Pope issued his condemnation of the new religious order (throwing in, for good measure, a denunciation of all the liberal and egalitarian principles of the Revolution), the split was already complete. In accordance with the principles of religious freedom, the non-juring clergy and their followers had the same rights as any sect, and accommodating constitutional priests were sometimes willing to share the use of the parish churches. But feelings were already embittered on both sides of the divide. The regime of toleration lasted about six months, during which time revolutionary militants broke up non-juring congregations in Paris and other cities, while in many country areas the people remained faithful to their old priests, and the newcomer ('the intruder') was insulted, beaten up, or completely ignored. Discontent with the new regime was spreading among peasants and artisans in 1791 and 1792, and wherever this happened the malcontents identified themselves with the non-juring clergy and seized on the symbols of traditional Catholicism. Meanwhile, the revolutionary avant-garde, drawn mainly from the lower middle class of the towns, was becoming increasingly self-confident and aggressive. The first measures against 'refractory priests' came in late 1791, with the outbreak of war against Austria in April 1792, and more especially after the enemy invasion in July, witch-hunts became the order of the day, and non-juring priests were the most accessible targets. In September there were 200 priests among the prisoners murdered in Paris at the height of the invasion scare. As France dissolved in civil war during 1793 many hundreds more were shot, drowned or guillotined, or knifed to death. At the same time, the Revolution began to turn against its friends in the constitutional church.

As it became clear that the constitutional church was not the church of the nation, but one sect among many, there was a growing trend towards the development of a civic ritual without church support. In 1790, the anniversary of the taking of the Bastille had been the occasion for the erection of altars of the Fatherland, before which public officials came for a mass swearing of loyalty. In Provence, three quarters of the communes holding such ceremonies preceded the oath-taking with a mass; in 1791, only half included a mass; in 1792 only a fifth. Meanwhile, ardent 'patriots', as the champions of the new order were known, were bringing their children to those altars for civic baptism. In 1792, the year of the outbreak of war and the fall of the monarchy, the movement away from the official church gathered force. In some southern towns, such as Marseille, republican jokers processed through the streets dressed as priests and monks, carrying mock relics and leading mitred donkeys. Similar orgies of ridicule had marked the early stages of the Protestant Reformation; now they signalled the beginnings of a new Reformation, in which Christianity itself was the target. In September a big step towards a secular state was taken in the introduction of civil marriage and divorce, in spite of the opposition of the state clergy. By January 1793 the constitutional bishop of Clermont-Ferrand, who had just lost his position as president of the departmental council, was complaining in a pastoral letter that: 'Some deeply corrupted men have conspired against the Lord and his Christ. Under the specious pretext of freedom of opinion, they are destroying all morality, undermining the foundations of all virtue, annihilating all principles of sociability . . . Extravagance is carried to the point of saying that no God is needed, no public worship, no religion . . .'[2]

In March the peasants of the Vendée rose against the Revolution, non-juring priests at their sides and badges depicting the Sacred Heart of Jesus on their coats. In June many constitutional clergy were involved in the 'federalist' risings against the authority of Paris in such towns as Lyon, Marseille and Bordeaux. As the Revolution entered its most radical phase in the second half of 1793 there was a widespread demand for a complete break with the past. In October a new calendar was introduced, which counted the years from the establishment of the French Republic in September 1792. Later in the month the programme of forcible dechristianisation began, initiated sometimes by the local popular society, sometimes by the representative on mission of the Committee of Public Safety in Paris or by the revolutionary armies, volunteer militia recruited in the cities for the purpose of securing food supplies and rooting out counter-revolutionaries in the surrounding countryside. These revolutionary stalwarts tended to see 'fanatics' (as the jargon for 'practising Christian' became) lurking beneath every bed. Not only could the Vendée and the federalist revolt be blamed on them: even peasant grain-hoarders were suspected of being under the influence of unpatriotic priests. So the sansculottes of the Year II of Liberty tried to rebuild the nation's shattered unity by destroying its Catholic traditions.

The new focus of authentic religious and moral feeling, irreproachably republican and untouched by aristocratic hand, was to be the cult of Reason and Liberty, celebrated from November 1793 until it was superseded by the cult of the Supreme Being in May 1794. All over France churches became Temples of Reason, and beautiful teenage girls of good republican family acted as goddess of Reason or of Liberty. (Conservative propaganda later suggested that the principal actresses in these earnest celebrations had been prostitutes; but the White Terrorists of 1795 recognised the true seriousness of this attempt to harness the religious feeling of the people for new republican purposes when they murdered two girls who had acted as goddesses in a Festival of Reason at Marseille.) Meanwhile heavy pressure was put on the constitutional clergy to abdicate. Many did so, including about half of the bishops, so that the already serious shortage of priests became yet more acute – though some continued to live in their parishes, and perform Catholic rites privately, at the request of their parishioners.

Relief came for the hard-pressed Catholics of France through the ninth Thermidor (the coup of 27 July 1794), which restored the dominance of the moderate bourgeoisie. Not that they were any more Catholic than their sansculotte predecessors: but they were less concerned about moulding the new revolutionary man. Their solution to the religious problem was the formal separation of church and state, and the freedom to worship behind closed doors – though not to ring bells or process through the streets. Slowly churches began to reopen, and priests began to come out of hiding or return from exile, though the evident link between the orthodox Catholic clergy and reviving royalist feeling led to further restrictions on the clergy between 1797 and 1799. By 1796 many parts of France were in the grip of a religious revival. In parts of the west and the south-east there had been a continuity of Catholic royalist feeling since the first years of the Revolution. Now, in areas where dechristian-isation had seemed triumphant in the Year II, women especially were demanding the reopening of the churches and still illegal processions and pilgrimages were starting again. As Olwen Hufton puts it: 'Citoyenne Defarge, ex-*tricoteuse*, put down her needles and reached for her rosary beads.'[3] Even in 1794 many clergy had risked arrests for 'fanaticism' by holding well-attended clandestine services; and where priests were not available, villagers broke into their churches and persuaded a school-teacher or a gravedigger or a farmer to say mass on Easter Sunday. But it seems that in 1795 and 1796, famine, and weariness with the Revolution, and the feeling that the sufferings of the people were perhaps a punishment for their rejection of the church, may have added a new dimension to popular Catholicism. In Bayeux bread rioters had the slogan 'When God was here we had bread'. At the opposite end of

France, in the Hérault, bells were beginning to ring again in these years (in spite of the law), crucifixes and medallions were being worn, confraternities reconstituted. By 1799 Corpus Christi processions were again being held in many parts of the south. According to Cholvy: 'The three years (1798–1801) preceding the signature of the Concordat are those of a general explosion in favour of Catholic worship. They leave the authorities increasingly impotent.'[4]

In the person of Napoleon the authorities finally recognised this fact. After the settlement of 1801, the church could at last set about the work of reconstruction.

II

Forced dechristianisation failed therefore to wean France's millions of 'fanatics' from their 'gothic superstitions'. Like all such campaigns, it caused vast amounts of unnecessary suffering, and like most of them it was largely counter-productive. It did however make apparent religious divisions that already existed beneath the surface, which have, to quite a large degree, persisted until the present day. It is clear that dechristianisation was not merely imposed from above, and was not solely an expedient of national defence, as historians from both the Jacobin and the Catholic traditions have tended to suggest. It expressed the accumulated resentment against church and clergy of many sections of the population. This violent rejection of Catholicism was mainly an urban phenomenon, but it took both bourgeois and more popular forms. And the events of the 1790s made it equally clear that the countryside included both areas of fervent Catholicism, and those where the church was a much more peripheral feature of life.

The first sign of these deep divisions within the religious life of France was the varying response to the oath of loyalty imposed on the clergy at the end of 1790. The higher clergy generally refused on class grounds to take it. Several bishops had emigrated already, and before long many others did so. But the parish clergy split about equally. In towns, non-jurors were usually in a majority, but in the countryside the proportion of jurors varied enormously. At one extreme was the Var, now among the least devout of French departments, where 96 per cent took the oath. In the still solidly Catholic Morbihan it was a mere 10 per cent. This was the most striking aspect of the pattern of acceptance and refusal: the non-juring strongholds tended to be those rural areas where Catholic practice is highest today, while juring areas, like the centre and the south-east were those where the church is now weak. The explanation seems to lie in the fact that rural priests were strongly affected in their decisions by the views of their parishioners, and that the attitude of the rural population to the Civil Constitution was affected both by their reaction to the proposed diminution in the social role of the clergy and by their judgement of the Revolution in general. It seems that enthusiasm for the Revolution tended to be strongest in those social classes and in those regions where the hold of the Catholic church was relatively weak. The events of the Revolution greatly exacerbated this tendency by further alienating 'patriots' from the church, and strengthening the Catholic loyalties of those who saw the Revolution as merely a regime of famine, terror and war.

So far as social classes were concerned, the group which gained most from the Revolution, the bourgeoisie, was often luke-warm in its Catholicism, while the most devout class, the peasantry, was also that which gained least (the aristocracy excepted). Meanwhile the artisans tended either towards ultra-radicalism or counter-revolution, and the poorest sections of the population were largely isolated both from the church and from regular political activity.

The divisions within rural France can be seen in microcosm in the Maine-et-Loire *département*. In the Loire valley and the area round Saumur, the majority of the clergy took the oath; in the remoter Mauges, only 8 per cent did so. In the former area there was widespread enthusiasm for the Revolution, the Civil Constitution of the clergy provoked little opposition, and the counter-revolutionary movement gained little support; the Mauges, on the other hand, would become a stronghold of counter-revolution, and it was the Civil Constitution which provided the first focus for a mounting discontent with the new regime. Behind these differing responses to the political and ecclesiastical changes of the Revolution were considerable differences in social structure. The more concentrated, more market-oriented and less remote population of the Saumurois was more accessible to new ideas, more under the influence of the bourgeoisie, and – because of the tendency of large monastic estates to concentrate in these more prosperous areas – more anti-clerical. On the other hand, the slogans of the Revolution awakened less interest in the isolated communities of the Mauges; the bourgeoisie were both less influential and more resented; there was less hostility to the aristocracy; and the clergy were the leaders of their people in a way that was relatively uncommon in the more developed and socially heterogeneous Saumurois.

The Mauges was typical of those parts of France which gained little from the Revolution. The limitation of the franchise to 'active citizens' excluded the great majority of peasants and artisans; both groups resented the bourgeois domination of the new local authorities, and the fact that political authority became much more obtrusive than it had been under the old regime; the hoped-for reduction in taxes never came; and further discredit was cast on the Revolution in peasant eyes by the decision of the Constituent Assembly to compensate the landlords for the loss of feudal dues. In an area of hamlets and scattered farmhouses, the parish church was the symbol of community, confraternities were among the main meeting-points, and the parish priest enjoyed enormous influence and respect. In the Mauges, the Civil Constitution of the clergy was seen as an attack on this influence and it was bitterly resented. Support for the 'good priests' was the issue which served more than any other in 1791 to crystallise opposition to the new regime, and to form a general mood of resistance that would culminate in armed insurrection in 1793. The Civil Constitution excluded the clergy from many public offices, and transferred some of their powers (notably control over charity) to local authorities, dominated by an often anti-clerical bourgeoisie, which tended to see the clergy as rivals. The many rural communes that had elected their priest as mayor naturally preferred to keep a leader whom they trusted; and the poorer members of the population feared that the secularisation of charity would merely mean less charity; piety and envy equally led the peasants to condemn the wealthy minority who managed to buy church lands – most of them bourgeois, and often leading 'patriots'. In such places, priests who condemned the Civil Constitution were assured of a respectful hearing, but often it was the people who applied the pressure; one Breton *curé* who took the oath complained that 'The people treated me like an intruder, though I have occupied my functions for forty years.'[5] So when the non-juring priests were ejected from their parishes, only the committed supporters of the new order continued to attend the parish church. While the churches were emptying, large crowds were gathering at isolated chapels or in the open air for services conducted by their old priests, in which a fervid traditional Catholicism mixed with a total condemnation not only of the new religious order, but of the 'patriots' and their Revolution.

If the events of the Revolution strengthened the religious loyalties of many, they also seem to have hastened the trend towards religious indifference in some parts of France. By the 1770s and 1780s half or more of the population were failing to do their Easter Duties in the larger towns, in some villages and small towns, including the Bordeaux region, and the river ports south from Paris. In the coastal areas of Languedoc there seems to be clear evidence of a decline during the eighteenth century. All of these were areas marked by Catholic weakness and sometimes advanced dechristianisation in the nineteenth century. All were areas where the constitutional church predominated in the 1790s. The new regime of religious freedom encouraged the luke-warm to abandon any remaining religious practice; the long closure of churches and absence of priests enabled some to lose their church-going habits; and it seems that others were sick of the bitter conflict between constitutional and Roman clergy and decided, as the constitutional bishop of Rouen complained, 'to stay neutral': 'Meanwhile the children grow without instruction, confession or first communion, and consequently marry without priestly blessing'.[6] In Montpellier Easter 1791 had seen a big drop in the number of communicants, and in Bayeux, the majority of the population stopped going to mass between Christmas 1791 and Easter 1792 – and never returned. As Bishop Grégoire, leader of the constitutional church tried to pick up the pieces again, after the holocaust of 1793–4, his colleagues reported similar situations in many parts of central and northern France. In the Saône-et-Loire a parish priest reported in 1800 that his parishioners showed 'a public and shameful contempt for everything that belongs to religion – the sanctification of Sundays and feast days, attendance at divine service, participation in the sacred mysteries, frequentation of the sacraments', a contempt which he blamed on the perversion of religion by the refractory priests. From the Marne came complaints of the apathy of the rural population: the churches were reopening, but the villagers were in no hurry to return to them, and in Amiens the bishop claimed that Sundays and Feast days had lost their religious significance.[7]

But though the Revolution opened for many the way to religious indifference, it also initiated the great war between Catholic France and anti-clerical France that was to dominate the history of the nineteenth century. This anti-clerical France included an influential minority of Protestants – and in some areas the Revolution was a continuation of the Wars of Religion. But in most areas it was led by ex-Catholics, deist or atheist, who had come to hate the religion in which they had been brought up, seeing in it a stronghold of superstition, authoritarianism and reaction.

The violent dechristianisation of the Year II brought together two quite different currents of anti-Catholic feeling, the one drawing on the 'philosophy' of the eighteenth century Enlightenment, and the other stemming from traditions of popular anti-clericalism. The connecting thread between them was the belief that Christianity nourished the forces of political reaction.

The 'philosophical' current drew on a critique of Reformation and Counter-Reformation religious orthodoxies which had its origins in England and Holland in the later seventeenth century, but which reached its fullest development in France around the middle of the eighteenth century. This critique had begun as a revisionist movement within the Calvinist churches; by the end of the seventeenth century it was frequently taking a deistic form; by the mid-eighteenth it was sometimes atheistic. In France censorship severely limited the publication and distribution of unorthodox literature until at least the middle of the eighteenth century, but by the 1720s there was an extensive trade based mainly in Holland in the production and export to France of banned books. The cardinal point of this attack on existing religious orthodoxies was a rejection of the claims of Christianity, or any other revealed religion, to offer an exclusive and conclusive knowledge of the will of God and the destiny of man. Instead, the 'philosophy' of the eighteenth century insisted that it was only through the use of their reason that human beings could make sense of the world around them and formulate rules for living, and that the dictates of reason should override the prescriptions of tradition or of religious authority wherever these came into conflict. The basic source of human misery, it was argued, lay not in original sin, but in ignorance, and through reason, science, education, most of these miseries could be removed. Together with reason, the other safe guide for human conduct was nature: nature commanded that earthly happiness be pursued, that the good things of life be enjoyed, and pain and suffering avoided wherever possible. The best model for the good life was offered neither by the hedonist nor the ascetic, but by the good citizen, a parent and a loyal and public-spirited member of his community, tolerant, rational, abreast of modern culture.

In its more extreme form this movement of religious rationalism was represented by the thorough-going materialism of the *curé* Meslier (who died in 1729, leaving a Testament which was to anticipate many of the arguments of modern atheism). More widely influential was the liberalised religion of those like Rousseau, who asserted belief in a benevolent Creator, revealing himself through nature, whose commands were in perfect accord with human reason. Whether atheist, deist or liberal Christian, the Enlightenment meant a repudiation of many aspects of Tridentine Catholicism, and usually a suspicion of clerical pretensions and resistance to any attempt to limit religious freedom in the interests of religious orthodoxy. There is in fact a fair amount of evidence for an increasing secularisation of many areas of French life between 1750 and 1789, a period that conveniently begins with the *Encyclopaedia*, the most influential synthesis of Enlightenment orthodoxies, and coincides with the time when the prestige of the French 'philosophers' was at its highest. It is not yet clear, however, what the connection between this apparent secularisation and the concurrent climax of the French Enlightenment was. For instance, Vovelle's work on Marseille shows a substantial decline in the course of the eighteenth century, and more especially from 1750 onwards, in the proportion of babies baptised on their day of birth, the proportion of testators asking for masses to be said for them after their death, and the proportion of wills including extensive pious references. But in the case of requests for masses, where highly detailed figures are available, there is such a close correspondence between the figures for members of the liberal professions and those for the most illiterate group (peasants), that it seems improbable that philosophy can provide the major explanation of the decline.[8]

However, there can be no doubt that Enlightenment ideas influenced the religious policies of the revolutionary assemblies from 1789 onwards, and the dechristianising initiatives of some of the representatives on mission in 1793–4. No doubt most members of the Constituent Assembly would have called themselves Catholics, and only in 1792 would some of France's legislators frankly declare themselves unbelievers. But the religion of many of these bourgeois Catholics was different in some significant respects from that of the majority of the clergy. The Constituent Assembly was guided by utilitarian considerations in planning its reform of the church. The church in their view existed to serve the people: so 'useless' elements, such as contemplative monks and nuns should be eliminated; the structure of the church should be rationalised, without any regard for continuity with the past; and since the people (or at least that small section of the people who qualified as 'active citizens') were the best judges of their own interests, they must select their own pastors. In line with the anti-sectarian and anti-dogmatic bias of the Enlightenment, they removed all the legal protection offered to Catholicism and the disabilities suffered by non-Catholics, but rejected the idea that any religious test be applied to those voting in the new church elections. With complete disregard for the susceptibilities of the clergy, the Assembly imposed the Civil Constitution as a *fait accompli*, denying the church even the degree of very limited autonomy that it had enjoyed under the old regime.

The Constituent Assembly tried – and failed – to modernise the church. Only in 1792 and 1793 did those come to the fore who wanted a total remaking of France's religious institutions on the basis of Enlightenment principles. One example was Couthon, a close associate of Robespierre, and representative on mission in the Puy-de-Dôme at the time of the dechristianisation. A Rousseauist deist, he was equally opposed to atheism and to orthodox Christianity. Believing that man is born good, but is corrupted by bad institutions, he saw the church as one of these harmful influences. He bitterly opposed the existence of a priesthood, seeing it as a threat to freedom, and he objected to any kind of public worship, arguing that God desires 'no altar but the heart of his children, no temple but the world of which he is the Architect'. As far as public policy was concerned, his main objection was to any kind of state support for, or recognition of, Catholicism; only when the dechristianisation movement had already begun did he come round to support the use of force – until then he had assumed that 'philosophy' alone would defeat the Catholic church and clergy.

The popular anti-clericalism of the revolutionary 1790s also had pre-revolutionary precedents, admittedly much less spectacular. For instance, investigations in Languedoc have provided details of the prolonged conflicts between monastic landlords and the local population, and of the harassment by youth groups of priests who tried to attack the established patterns of leisure.

In some respects this popular anti-clericalism looks like a branch of the war between the sexes. In 1793–4 it was generally men who took the lead in closing the churches, and often women who tried to keep them open. In Paris, at least, it seems that there was already a difference between the religious practice of men and women before 1789. Attacks on the church were in part an attack on a world where women escaped from the direct control of their husbands, and attacks on the clergy were partly a product of male jealousy. The representative on mission in the Gers told a crowd of women that they were all 'priests' prostitutes'. At a time when religion seemed to be nourishing counter-revolution this part-independence of women was doubly dangerous. As an official from Toulouse told the popular society of a Tarn commune in January 1794: 'The men made the Revolution, and it was not for the women to undo their work.'[9]

The new factor in the 1790s was the belief that a general emancipation from the Catholic church, and indeed from Christianity of any kind, was possible, and that the ideals of the Revolution provided an all-sufficient programme for the regeneration of humanity. From this perspective the clergy were at best trying to serve two masters – God and the Revolution. The Vendée would suggest that these two masters were actually opposed. The roots of the revolutionary dechristianisation are to be sought not so much in the action of the church as in the increasingly religious character of the Revolution itself, and the fact that Catholicism came to be seen as a rival and, in some respects, incompatible faith. So that when in September 1792 the *curé* of St. Laurent in Paris held a service in memory of the 'martyrs of the 10th August', the assembly of the Poissonière section rejected an invitation to attend in the following terms:

It is time at last to speak the language of reason. . . . The martyrs of liberty, our brave brothers who died on the 10th of August, have no need, sir, of being excused or recommended to a just, good and merciful God. . . . God is just, sir, and consequently our brothers enjoy a perfect happiness which nothing can disturb. Only bad citizens can doubt that. Show us on your altars the glorious victims of Liberty, crowned with flowers, taking the place of St Crispin and St Cucufin.[10]

Thus, without as yet specifically rejecting Christianity, the sansculottes were replacing Catholic categories with others of their own making, of which salvation by politics alone was one. With the murder of Marat in July 1793 the new religion found its exemplary man. Within a few days he was being compared to Jesus Christ, and in the autumn the old Catholic processions were replaced by processions through the streets of Paris headed by statues of the 'trinity' of revolutionary martyrs, Marat, Chalier and Le Peletier.

In some areas new republican forms seem to have been given to beliefs whose essential content remained unchanged – in much the same way that Christian saints once took over from pagan deities. So that in two western *départements* republican girls murdered by counter-revolutionary terrorists became revolutionary saints, and the places of their deaths were marked by shrines, where miracles were said to be frequent. In Paris, Soboul suggests, the cult of Marat was interpreted by the people as a new form of the old cult of the saints.[11] But beyond this simple substitution, there was on the part of many republicans in this Year II of Liberty a passionate concern with propagating the Truth, and with confronting old error at every point, regardless of political expediency. Thus in September 1793 one Parisian section was claiming that the greatest danger was 'not the league of tyrants allied against liberty, but the league of fanatics allied against reason'. It called for the establishment in every canton of adult schools, where 'horror of fanaticism' would be preached every Sunday and saint's day; a month later the district of Compiègne was putting some of these ideas into practice by suppressing religious teaching in the municipal secondary school and replacing it with study of the Rights of Man (a document to which, in fact, many beleaguered 'fanatics' were making vain appeal at this time) and the Constitution of 1793.[12] The most striking symbol of this wholesale rejection of France's Christian past was the new calendar, adopted in October 1793, which counted its years, not from the birth of Jesus, but from the abolition of the French monarchy in 1792, and which attempted to kill two birds with one stone by extending the working week from six days to nine, and replacing the Sunday with a *décadi*. Not surprisingly, the latter idea never really caught on, but when Napoleon finally returned to the old calendar, one real improvement was lost: the superbly evocative new names for the months, such as *ventôse* and *germinal*. The most devastating measure of dechristianisation was perhaps the secularisation of the cemeteries, affronting as it did the most deeply felt part of popular Catholicism. As a song current in 1794 in Normandy complained: 'They lead a body to the grave, without saying a prayer for it. They leave it to rot in the ground like a Huguenot.'[13]

III

The Concordat between Napoleon and Pope Pius VII was signed in 1801 and came into force in 1802. The Pope wanted the official recognition of the Roman Catholic religion by the government of the most powerful Christian nation and the repudiation of the constitutional church. Napoleon wanted the reunification of France's divided Catholics and an effective system of government control. Napoleon got what he wanted through the provisions that the bishops would be nominated by the government, the parish clergy by the bishops, and both would be paid by the state. The Pope, though soon drawn into bitter conflict with Napoleon, had gained the two essential points, and would come fully into his own after the restoration of the Bourbons in 1814. The main victim of the Concordat was the constitutional church, and thus the alliance between church and Revolution of which its priests were the leading exponents. While Napoleon wanted a complete integration of former jurors and non-jurors in the reorganised church, only sixteen of the first sixty bishops nominated were constitutionals, and they naturally did not include the more politically radical among them, such as bishop Grégoire of Blois, who was to remain a republican and democrat, and an outspoken critic of successive French governments until his death in 1831. Meanwhile, at parish level, any such integration was made difficult by the animosity that existed between jurors and non-jurors; and it was often made impossible by reactionary bishops, who were determined to have their revenge on the 'schismatics', and who by requiring of the constitutionals a public repudiation of the Civil Constitution, followed by an act of penance, ensured that many of them stayed out in the cold. In those areas where the constitutional clergy had predominated, the result was a repetition of the conflicts of 1791 between incumbent and 'intruder' – with the roles reversed. Just as in 1791, the newcomer sometimes had to enter his parish flanked by an armed guard, and once established he might face a boycott from parishioners loyal to their old priest, who might continue to say mass, and administer the sacraments on private premises. The official pastor would hit back by refusing to bury those who were known to attend the rival services, and even those who had been married by a 'schismatic' before the Concordat and had failed to go through a new ceremony. Unlike the 'right-wing' critics of the Concordat, who formed their own breakaway organisations, known collectively as the 'Petite Eglise', the 'unreconciled' constitutionals remained a large number of unorganised individuals, hoping for eventual reintegration into the national church. Over the next two or three decades some were reconciled with their bishops, others died, and they had no successors. But they left powerful memories behind them, and studies both of the Rennes and the Montpellier dioceses suggest that areas with large numbers of 'unreconciled' constitutionals became strongholds of nineteenth-century anti-clericalism.[14] The supporters of the constitutional church thus tended to join those 'patriots' who were already alienated from the Catholic church. And whereas in the 1790s devout Catholics had been completely divided in their politics, a combination of sansculotte terrorism and the policies of the church's new leaders was laying the basis for a clear-cut distinction between a Catholic Right and an anti-clerical Left.

Meanwhile, the experiences of the 1790s had confirmed most of the non-juring clergy in a hatred of the Revolution, and a preference for monarchy. The Concordat fairly effectively bought their acquiescence in the Napoleonic regime. But the Emperor's relations with the clergy were always strained, and there can have been few former 'refractories' who did not cheer the return of the Bourbons. As far as their loyal parishioners were concerned, the years of persecution had strengthened the bond between priest and people, and laid the basis for Catholic and conservative traditions that have sometimes lasted to the present day.

Cholvy in his monumental study of religion in the Hérault notes that while in some parishes the 1790s were the high point of a history of violent anti-clericalism that began before the Revolution and continued long after:

Other parishes would carefully maintain the tradition – transmitted by the old people to the children during the long evening gatherings (*veillées*) of former years – of their faithfulness to the good priests, of the ruses that were used to hide them, of the masses celebrated in the forest, in caves or in barns. When Jacques Bel, *curé* of St Gervais-sur-Mare in the Espinouze, returned to his parish in 1803, after ten years of a wandering life that took him first to Italy and then since 1795 to the mountains near his parish, his parishioners gave him an immense reception. They went to meet him waving flags and banging drums.[15]

As for the aristocracy: in the later years of the *ancien régime*, religion had been out of fashion, but already in the later 1790s there were the first signs of a return to the church. Under the Restoration, the aristocracy generally became strong supporters of the Catholic church and of clerical power. Many individuals underwent some kind of personal conversion; but regardless of individual conviction, the aristocracy as a class became committed to the defence of the church as a social and political institution, and this relationship continued right through the nineteenth century. In these years, the victims of the Revolution made common cause, each convinced that only the alliance of throne, altar and château could avert a second catastrophe.

IV

Similar alliances were formed in most other west European countries during the revolutionary wars and the period of reactionary rule that followed Napoleon's final defeat in 1815. In these years the demand for religious freedom and equality was a central part of any programme for the democratisation and liberalisation of society. On the conservative side, orthodox religion became the essential link between traditional elites and their peasant or proletarian followers – and thus, in radical eyes, 'the opium of the people'. Among the forces of progress, dissenting religion was often an equally important link between leaders and led: Nonconformist chapels, Freemasons' lodges or freethinking groups were political bases, and attacks on the official clergy were the radical orator's most trusted stock-in-trade.

Thus, between the officially enforced religious unity of the *ancien régime* and the pluralism of the present era, there came Europe's age of religious polarisation. This took several different forms. The most familiar pattern is that established in France during and after the Revolution. Here, as the Roman Catholic church became committed to the restoration of the old order, all liberal, radical, and socialist movements acquired a sharp anti-clerical edge. In particular, control of the national school system was bitterly contested between the clergy and their enemies. The same happened in most other homogeneously Catholic countries during the nineteenth century. In these countries working-class socialists inherited the militant anti-clericalism of the old middle-class Left, so that religion continued to be an essential issue between Right and Left even when parties were ostensibly defined by the economic interests of their supporters. In 1926 an analysis of Austrian politics would still argue that the Catholic church was 'the real enemy of Socialism': 'She is the upholder of conservatism, loyalty, piety, respect and obedience, the supporter, incidentally, of country against town, and Gentile against Jew. Until her hold over the spirits of the people has been weakened, Socialism, the very reverse of all this, cannot move.'[16] And it was in the 1930s that the conflict between clerical and anti-clerical in Catholic Europe reached its horrifying climax in the Spanish civil war, where it is estimated that 0.5 per cent of the nuns, 12 per cent of the monks, 13 per cent of the secular priests and 20 per cent of the bishops in Spain were executed by the Republicans. After the Nationalist victory, the close alliance between the church and Franco, which lasted into the 1960s, helped to give continuing life to the anti-clerical obsession: in 1958 a study of a Madrid parish claimed that when workers met in a bar they would take the opportunity of working off some of their frustration by a 'constant and merciless criticism of everything which signifies civil or religious authority'.[17]

A second pattern, seen most clearly in Britain, though a similar situation existed in Sweden, was that in which a conservative established church was pitted against a variety of dissenting forces, including Roman Catholics and secularists, but with Protestant sectarians in the leading role. Here church v. chapel was an essential part of the battle between the old order and its enemies, and the numerous Protestant sects often had a clearly marked social and political identity. Here again education was a major arena of conflict.

In England too the 1790s were years of revolution – but of defeated revolution. The first enthusiastic response to 1789 came from middle class religious dissenters, who launched an abortive campaign for the removal of their disabilities. But, beginning in Sheffield in late 1791, there followed a much more widespread movement of artisan and petit bourgeois radicalism, inspired by the French sansculottes and the writings of Tom Paine. It won a first great accession of support in late 1792, while the First Republic was being established in Paris, and a second in the hunger year of 1795; it collapsed under the weight of successive waves of repression in 1796. But by then democratic and anti-clerical ideas had taken deep root among the artisans of such cities as London, Sheffield and Norwich, and among the weavers of the Pennines; no persecution succeeded in eradicating these ideas, and they were to hold a dominant influence over the politically-conscious workers at many points in the nineteenth century.

The special significance of the 1790s in England's religious history is two-fold: it was in these years that deism and atheism first established a popular following, usually in close alliance with democratic politics; and, of greater immediate importance, they also saw a tremendous growth of Protestant dissent. In these years we see the first signs of nineteenth-century England's characteristic religious pattern: the division between a conservative state church, a liberal Protestant dissent, and a radical secularism. The assault on the *ancien régime* had both a religious and a secularist wing, and the religious wing was much the stronger.

The conflict between church and chapel was most intense between about the 1830s and the 1880s. In small towns and large villages it could be all-pervasive, whereas in larger towns there was more scope for indifference, and in smaller villages squires could often impose a political and religious consensus. In a market town and centre of artisan production like Banbury, with a population of 10,000 at the middle of the nineteenth century, there was a Tory/Anglican bank and a Liberal/ Nonconformist bank, church shops and chapel shops; in 1857 two rival corn exchanges were built.[18] At the head of the chapel party were both those whose Nonconformist ancestry went back for many generations, and who, however wealthy they might be, suffered exclusion from the political and social élite on religious grounds, and others, usually upwardly mobile, whose conversion to Nonconformity was fairly recent. Municipal reform in 1835 often meant that this new élite was able to replace long-established Anglican wealth, sometimes with strong 'county' associations, at the head of town government. Behind the relatively moderate leadership of the chapel party, interested mainly in enjoying a share of power and recognition, there was often a larger body of more militant shopkeepers and craftsmen, whose religious dissent was part of a more general programme for the democratisation of society. On both the church and chapel side there was also an extensive clientele of those employed by the leaders of the rival party or dependent on their custom. Through the middle decades of the nineteenth century, and more especially in the 1850s, 1860s and 1870s, with the decline of Chartism, these were the lines on which the battle for local power was fought, and according to which the voters aligned themselves in parliamentary elections. During these years education policy was mainly debated in sectarian terms, and issues concerned with the privileges of the established churches or the rights of religious dissenters were continually at the forefront of politics, and provided the clearest line of distinction between Tories on the one hand and Whigs/Radicals/Liberals on the other. Meanwhile, those offering more general challenges to the land-owning class, from the wealthy industrialists of the Anti-Corn Law League to the impoverished labourers of the farm workers' union, often found their most effective advocates in Nonconformist preachers.

A third pattern of politico-religious conflict is that found in Germany and the Netherlands. Here the mobilisation of the previously passive majority took the form of what the Dutch call *verzuiling*, the formation of a series of discrete sub-cultures, each living a life largely separated from that of the others, each represented by its own political parties, and each having its own characteristic religious institutions. In the Netherlands a frightened monarch had in 1848 conceded a liberal constitution with a limited franchise. For the first three decades of the new regime politics were dominated by the liberals. But from the late 1870s three major groups began to organise themselves in opposition to the ruling group, which was drawn mainly from the business and professional classes, and was in religious terms mostly liberal Protestant or agnostic: first the various bodies of militant Calvinists, who came together in the 1890s to form the *Gereformeerd* church, and whose political arm was the Anti-Revolutionary Party; then the large Roman Catholic minority; and finally the socialists. The principle objective of the ultra-Calvinists and of the Roman Catholics was state support for their own schools, which they obtained in 1889. They already had their own universities and daily papers. Soon they had their own trade unions, as of course did the socialists. A whole series of other organisations followed, even including a Catholic Goat Breeders' Association. As Kossmann defines it, '*Verzuiling* means that the state enables all the main groups of the population, Catholics, Protestants, socialists, humanists, etc., to organise their everyday life entirely as they wish: to have their own schools, youth associations, universities, sports' clubs, trade unions and employers' associations, their own social security organisations, and, for the cultural benefit of the masses, their own theatres, choirs, reading clubs, and, in the Netherlands, even their own broadcasting associations.'[19] One reflection of this politico-religious segregation of Dutch life was that in the 1950s various studies of rural areas, industrial areas, and even recently settled polders, showed that Catholics and ultra-Calvinists especially, and to a lesser extent other Protestants and those of no religion too, had a marked tendency to choose friends of their own religious or non-religious persuasion. It may also be an explanation for the fact that today considerably more people in the Netherlands than in any other west-European country, except for East Germany, declare themselves to be of no religion. The corollary of an exceptional level of sectarian consciousness and organisation seems to be an equally high level of organisation on the part of the non-religious, whether liberal humanists or socialists (the latter being very largely non-Christian until the Second World War).

The German Empire established in 1871 was a vastly more complex society than its tiny western neighbour, but they had certain points in common. One was the existence of a large and regionally concentrated Catholic minority (about 35 per cent of the German population in the later nineteenth century, concentrated in the south and west – about 40 per cent of the Dutch population, concentrated in the south). Another was the fact that political and economic power was far more heavily concentrated in Protestant hands than the balance of numbers might have led one to expect. A further point was that whereas the Catholic minority was fairly cohesive, the Protestants were politically and religiously divided. In the Netherlands many of the Protestant lower middle class and proletariat were alienated from the Dutch Reformed Church, and adhered either to the socialists or to the ultra-Calvinists. In Germany, sectarianism was less widespread, and before 1945 very few Protestants formally 'left the church', but only a minority of Protestants took much part in church life. A large part of the working class was socialist, and many of the middle class were religiously sceptical liberals. M.R. Lepsius argues that from 1871 until 1928 the German political system was dominated by four main groupings each having its basis in a distinct sub-culture; and that the party system was highly stable because each of the main parties had its own well-defined territory and found it difficult to recruit beyond it.[20] Two of these groups, the Catholics and the socialists, were defined by a shared religion or *Weltanschauung*. And the others, the conservatives and the liberals, were also fairly religiously homogeneous: the chief point held in common by the various groups supporting the Conservative Party was loyalty to the Protestant church; and the liberals were also mainly Protestant, but less orthodox or less devout in their religion. Socialists and Catholics, especially, tended to live most of their lives within a sectarian sub-culture. But the same was also true to a lesser extent of the conservatives and liberals, for whom Protestant organisations and the bourgeois *Vereine* respectively had the equivalent function of reinforcing a distinctive outlook on the world and isolating the believer from contact with those of other beliefs. Between 1929 and 1933 Protestant Germany polarised on class lines, but even then the Catholics remained a group apart, relatively immune to the pull of Nazis from the one side and Communists from the other, and, after 1945, able to rebuild a large part of their machinery for separate living.

The systems established in Germany and the Netherlands in the later nineteenth century were similar, but the results were widely different. In the Netherlands a fairly fluid system of shifting alliances between groups, none of which was strong enough to dominate the others, has produced a regime of peaceful though unfriendly co-existence. In Germany successive ruling groups have tried to assert unique legitimacy for their own sub-culture, and to win over the unconvinced majority by banning their organisations, imprisoning their leaders, censoring their newspapers, excluding them from state employment and indoctrinating their children. Under the Protestant monarchy which ruled from 1871 until 1918 it was Roman Catholics and socialists who found themselves under periodic attack, while church-going Protestants were preferred for state employment. Under the relatively liberal Weimar regime, most of the major political groupings used para-military organisations to coerce their opponents. Under the Nazis, all the institutions of the socialist sub-culture and most of those of the Protestants and Catholics were destroyed, and party members were encouraged to leave their churches. Under the Socialist Unity government in East Germany the churches' institutional network has been left substantially intact, but church membership is a disqualification for any position of power in society; while in the Federal Republic the same applies to membership of any organisation to the left of the Social Democrats.

There is a fourth pattern, which is familiar in eastern Europe, but in western Europe is more or less unique to Ireland – that is the situation where religion provided the fundamental basis for the identity, not of a class or a community, but of a nation. The Penal Laws of 1697–1703 had attempted, though with very slight success, to make the practice of the Roman Catholic religion impossible. Though these were repealed in 1782, Irish Catholics were denied political rights until 1829, and for long after that they remained economically subordinate. In these circum-stances religion provided the most important common reference point for the Catholics, who made up about three-quarters of the population, *vis-à-vis* the landowning class, the British generally, and the mass of poor Protestants in Ulster. Even in 1798, the rising of 'United Irishmen' which had been initiated by Protestants in the north took on a sectarian character in the south, where it included forced conversions of Protes-tants. All subsequent movements against British rule were to have a distinctly Catholic character, and though individual Protestants might be prominent within them, the Protestants as a body would oppose them. The earliest nation-wide movements – the campaigns for Catholic emancipation in the 1820s and for repeal of the union in the 1840s – depended heavily on the work of the clergy as local agents: and at elections, 'clerical intimidation successfully beat down and overpowered landlord intimidation.'[21] The other figures of power within the Catholic community tended to work in conjunction with the clergy, rather than becoming rivals to them. In the years of Catholic reconstruction after the repeal of the penal laws, new church buildings were a powerful symbol of the pride of the Catholic population. Meanwhile in the face of continuing disadvantages and grievances, the parish priest became, as a Fenian was to define it, 'the embodiment of hostility to England'. At many subse-quent points, and most notably during the period of Fenian risings and conspiracies in the 1860s, relations between the clergy and the revolutionary wing of Irish nationalism would be very strained. But there were very few Fenians, or other Irish revolutionaries, who abandoned their Catholic faith: it was too tightly bound up with their whole conception of what it meant to be Irish. Thus Catholicism and nationalism were mutually reinforcing, and the relationship continued to give the clergy a good deal of political influence, exerted with most effect to overthrow Parnell; but those Catholics who rejected the clergy's advice on politics usually remained loyal to the church according to their own understanding of it. When Ireland was partitioned in 1921 the line of division was basically that between predominantly Protestant areas and the rest of the country (though some predominantly Catholic areas remained in the United Kingdom against the wishes of their inhabitants). The resulting states both gave advantages to the majority confession: in the south this was reflected not only in the 'special position' of the Catholic church which the republican constitution of 1937 recognised, but more practically in legislation banning divorce and contraceptives, and instituting a system of censorship; in the north this meant the systematic discrimination against Catholics in such areas as public employment and housing. So the effect of the Irish political pattern was that both church loyalty and sectarian antagonism reached rare extremes, and organised secularism never gained the kind of support that it did in other parts of western Europe.

2 Social Cleavage

So, in the nineteenth century religion was itself a major source of conflict in west-European societies; it also reflected the other fundamental lines of division. The battles between the official churches and their opponents initially brought together coalitions of those from different social classes. But first in Britain, and then in almost every other country, social and political changes were tending to sharpen the antagonism between rich and poor, and to strengthen the class identities of both. The resulting conflicts would leave a decisive mark on the religious history of the nineteenth century and the first half of the twentieth.

The most obvious of these social changes was the population explosion. Between 1750 and 1850 the population increased by three times in Britain; it doubled in the Low Countries and Scandinavia; it increased by about 50 per cent in France and Portugal, and by more in Spain; there were also considerable increases in the German-speaking countries. What this could mean where individual welfare depended predominantly or overwhelmingly on access to land was shown in most extreme form in Ireland, where from 1750 to 1840 the population had grown as fast as in Great Britain, only to fall by a fifth in the famine decade of the 1840s. The famine followed several decades in which holdings were subdivided, the number of landless families grew, and an ever-increasing section of the rural population lived in severe poverty. Everywhere dramatic population growth without any corresponding increase in the land available meant a growing gulf between the large landowner or tenant farmer, able to profit from cheap labour and rising demand for food, and the growing number of impoverished smallholders and rural labourers. Even in Britain, where the development of industry offered the possibility of migration, the population of the countryside continued to increase in the early nineteenth century, reaching a peak around 1850. For the church the population explosion created two problems. One was the need to find the resources to build a mass of new churches and schools, and to pay the priests who would minister to this swelling population. More fundamentally, the growth in the numbers of the poor, and the increasing contrasts within the rural population were factors tending to exacerbate social antagonisms around the start of the nineteenth century, and to render increasingly difficult the attempts of the official churches to act as a focus of social unity.

The first half of the nineteenth century was a bad time for the poor of both town and countryside in many parts of Europe. Political and economic changes which in some instances brought some long term benefits brought in the short term nothing but increased suffering. The central development of these years was the rise to social dominance of the bourgeoisie in most parts of western Europe. In political terms this meant liberal legislation designed to lift all restrictions on the freedom of the market, and to produce a population of free, mobile, competitive individualists, in an economy founded on the principle of the sanctity of private property. Serfs were freed, feudal dues abolished in all those parts of western Europe where such institutions had persisted: but the compensation of landlords usually meant that the peasants were no better off financially after the emancipation than they had been before; and in some areas, notably eastern Germany, they ended up worse off. Church lands were sold all over Catholic Europe, beginning in Austria in the 1780s and ending in Italy in the 1860s: this time the main beneficiaries were the bourgeoisie, who in many parts of Spain, Portugal and Italy were able to establish huge estates, and once again the peasants gained little. In England, Scandinavia, and some parts of Germany the open fields were replaced by concentrated individual farms, and the commons and wastes were divided up between the proprietors of the parish – a victory, perhaps, for efficient farming, but a disaster for the cottagers who had grazed their animals on the commons, and for the squatters who were ejected from their homes and land. On the farms and in the textile industry improved machinery meant less work or none at all for half-starved labourers and weavers; governments repealed paternalistic legislation designed to protect particular categories of worker against the introduction of machinery, and when workers turned to breaking the machines they were imprisoned, transported or hanged. While economic changes, government policy and the population explosion were conspiring to increase the numbers of the very poor, measures such as England's New Poor Law of 1834 ensured that the authorities treated them more harshly. As agriculture in many parts of Europe, (with England and Scotland leading the way), was coming to be dominated by large-scale, profit-oriented landlords and farmers, the same process of concentration of economic power was gradually taking place in industry.

While some rural areas of western Europe remain to the present day islands of social peace and relative equality, all of the cities and industrial zones had seen by the early twentieth century a polarisation between a large propertyless working class and a small élite of large property owners, and most had gone through periods of serious conflict between these two groups. It was in England that the polarisation between a self-conscious middle class and working class first became a basic fact of life, and received its first classic statement (even starker than the facts themselves justified) in Engels's *Condition of the Working Class in England in 1844*. The working class included craftsmen, factory operatives, miners and unskilled labourers – still divided by differences of income, status and sectional interest, but united by a sense of common identity against the dominant class. In the mid-nineteenth century they made up the great majority of the population in the towns and industrial villages of England, and they still do. The middle class of urban and industrial England included a fairly numerous, but largely powerless section of shopkeepers, small employers and white collar workers, and a small élite of merchants, bankers, large employers and members of the exclusive professions, which merged at its upper reaches into the landowning class. From the late nineteenth century the lower middle class was the fastest growing group, and education began to provide a significant channel for upward mobility, but the basic contrast between a subordinate and disadvantaged mass and a small and largely hereditary élite remained, while the distinction between aristocracy and upper middle class became ever less significant. Important stages in the development of the situation described by Engels in the 1840s included the spread of factory industry, beginning with the mechanisation of cotton-spinning in Lancashire in the 1770s; the democratic movement of the 1790s, inspired by the French Revolution and the writings of Tom Paine, which established lasting traditions of artisan radicalism, and set large numbers of working men in stark opposition to a government that was determined to limit political rights to the holders of property; the *laissez-faire* legislation of 1809–14, which by repealing the laws that controlled apprenticeship, limited the use of machinery and empowered magistrates to impose minimum wages, hastened the decline of the craftsmen into a part of the general wage-earning class, and killed their faith in Parliament as then constituted; the consequent Luddite movement which, in its history of working-class destruction and ruling-class retribution, further hardened class antagonisms; the Peterloo Massacre of 1819, which became the most potent symbol of the disregard of the rich for the lives of the poor; and the most bitterly resented of the laws made in the years of middle-class triumph, the New Poor Law of 1834, with its policy of inducing the poor to work by making life intolerable for the 'able-bodied pauper'. The cumulative effect of these developments was to create more sharply defined classes of possessors and proletarians, and to alienate each from the other. The most obvious force for change was the apparently irresistible tendency towards the concentration of capital, meaning at least in the short run less social mobility, and towards the concentration of workers, facilitating class organisation. Yet as a factor in the developing alienation of class from class this was in itself less important than legislation which destroyed many of the paternalistic defences of the poor, while denying them any right to stand up for themselves in politics. While in the short run newly enrolled factory workers might well accept higher wages as a fair exchange for the noise, the heat and the harsh discipline of the factory, in the longer term, machinery, free trade, and the communications revolution meant that successive groups of workers faced wage-cuts, and lay-offs, and got caught in cycles of strike, lock-out and mutual terrorism, as their industries faced the full force of the national or international market. It was in the course of a thousand such local struggles that trade unionism and socialism were to root themselves in most of the industrial regions of Europe. The first victims of this process were to be in Lancashire itself, where in the 1790s the long decline of the handloom weavers began as a result of competition from worse-paid continental weavers using yarn spun in English mills. In the early decades of England's industrial revolution handloom weavers, rather than factory workers, would be the most radical section of the working class.

The poor expected their priests to speak out on their behalf. Some did. But, for the most part, during periods of acute social conflict in the nineteenth century, the official clergy identified with the possessors.

In rural England during the early nineteenth century this association was particularly close: the clergy were among the chief beneficiaries of the changes in these years. The enclosure acts which transformed large areas of central and eastern England between the 1750s and the 1830s, and which were so much resented by the rural poor, brought prosperity to many clergymen. Tithe-holders were usually awarded large amounts of land in commutation of tithe, and many superb Georgian rectories, towering above the houses of the parish, now more often occupied by stockbrokers than clergymen, were built on the proceeds. But the step which placed the parson on a level of equality with many squires, and helped to put him on friendlier terms with the farmers, tended to alienate him from the labourers. It was bad enough that the clergy were getting conspicuously richer at a time when the poor were getting poorer. To make matters worse many of them seemed to be putting on airs and mixing unwillingly with any but their social equals. Worst of all the clergy were becoming magistrates in large numbers at a time when the law was harsher and more class-biased than at any time before or since.

The reasons for the alliance of the official churches with the rich were complex and varied. This alliance was just as apparent in France as in England, though the French clergy mainly came from a peasant background and seldom stood to gain individually from the relationship. Here the church's response to the new social problems of the nineteenth century was partly determined by the principles that it had developed in opposition to the ideas of the French Revolution. In turning to help from monarchy and aristocracy in the face of the liberal threat, the Catholic church had formulated a view of human life in terms of which the hope of progress and of mass self-government was a delusion, inequality and suffering were necessary to the human condition, and the alternative to a democratic anarchy, which would soon become despotism, was the rule of a pious élite. In the mining district of the Pas-de-Calais, for instance, the clergy were not unaware of, or indifferent to, the sufferings of the workers: successive bishops of Arras, and many of the local clergy, condemned the exploitation of miners generally, or specific abuses. But they saw democracy or socialism as no answer: the answer was a more genuine paternalism. From this perspective the socialism that was gaining a hold over the working class at the end of the nineteenth century was a further development of the liberal heresy. Thus a diocesan official, reporting in 1877 on the progress of workmen's circles in the diocese of Arras, insisted on the importance of 'reacting against liberalism, radicalism and socialism, those three degrees of revolutionary error'.[1]

In explaining the predominance of this social conservatism, and the defeat of more radical alternatives, account has to be taken of the direct controls over the church exercised by the state and sometimes by landlords or industrialists; also of the need of clergymen with expensive building projects on their hands to cultivate wealthy patrons. Direct government controls included the nomination of bishops in England and France, and in Prussia appointment of the officials responsible for church discipline. In the 1840s, when many Prussian clergymen were calling for political liberalisation, and in the 1890s when some of them were championing the rights of workers, this control was used ruthlessly and effectively to ensure that the majority supported the government or remained politically passive. Meanwhile selection of parish ministers by landlords in many parts of England, Scotland and Germany ensured that conservatives found it easiest to obtain a parish. In the new industrial districts of France the anti-clerical policies of the republican governments in the 1880s and 1890s set up a vicious circle by which the church defended itself by becoming more reactionary: starved of funds by the government and unable to maintain the existing network of parishes, let alone establish new ones, the church turned for help to industrialists, in order to provide clergy and schools in areas of expanding population. Naturally this help was conditional: mine chaplains who criticised the company were dismissed; conversely, schools which stressed obedience, subordination and so on were generously supported.

In England the socially radical minority among the official clergy had more freedom of action than elsewhere. During the last quarter of the nineteenth century quite a large number of them were deliberately identifying themselves with their working-class parishioners. So, for instance, where the Chartists in the 1830s and 1840s had found the great majority of the Anglican parsons opposed to them, the dock strike of 1912 saw sixteen clergymen in the east London borough of Poplar, headed by the rector, declare their support for the strikers. Although the Anglican clergy remained predominantly Tory, the extremely decentralised system of patronage and the substantial autonomy enjoyed by parish incumbents meant that it was difficult to eliminate the dissident minority even where bishops wished to do so. In any case by the 1890s many bishops were prepared to give some encouragement to the new trend, in view of the evident alienation from the established church of large sections of the working class, and the need for new strategies in order to regain their support.[2]

The social radicalism of some of the English clergy in the late nineteenth century may have done something to ensure that the anti-clericalism of the growing labour movement remained a mild and peripheral affair. But it came too late to break the non-church-going habits of large sections of the working class, or the Nonconformist allegiance of most of those working-class people who were active church members. In nineteenth-century Europe periods of acute social tension frequently saw a large-scale alienation of the poor from the official churches. Most often they simply gave up attending services; sometimes they protested in a more active way by joining a Protestant sect or a secularist organisation, by seeking a civil marriage or demanding a secular burial.

In the course of the century the religious affiliations and practice of the cities and industrial zones of Europe came to be sharply differentiated by class. In most parts of France and Spain the rich Catholics went to mass while the poor stayed at home. Working-class Protestants also tended to desert the Protestant state churches, though quite a lot of them joined free churches. So, for instance, counts of church attendance in London in 1902–3 showed that Anglican congregations averaged 4 per cent of total population in the poorest districts, but 22 per cent in wealthy West End parishes. At this time the proportion of secular funerals varied from 7 per cent in the bourgeois 16th *arrondissement* of Paris to 39 per cent in proletarian Belleville.[3] In some countries the decline in middle-class religious practice made these contrasts less glaring; but in France and Spain enormous differentials continued into the 1950s and 1960s. In Lille, for instance, the proportion of mass-goers on a given Sunday ranged from 6 per cent of working-class adults to 51 per cent of those in the professional class; in Bordeaux it was 3 per cent and 32 per cent.

II

Yet some contemporaries thought that the class differences in religious life were less fundamental than the division between the religious outlook of men and women. In 1902 Drews began his account of religion in the big cities of Saxony: 'First of all the population divides itself into two great camps: the women are as a whole pious and church-oriented, but the world of men, busy with a thousand questions of life, is either completely indifferent to religious questions, or allows itself to be as religious as custom seems to require.'[4] Some fifty years later, in the completely different surroundings of an Andalusian rural community, Pitt-Rivers would make a very similar comment: 'The *pueblo* looks upon religion as women's business.'[5] This was in spite of the fact that the state-supported churches, and most of the major Protestant sects too, were dominated by men. In the Catholic church nuns generally had a big role in education and care of the sick; and in rural areas women in lay orders taught the catechism and conducted family prayers; but the priesthood remains to this day a male monopoly. The Protestant state churches have allowed women to become ministers only since the Second World War. In nineteenth-century Britain prophetesses and women evangelists were instrumental in the foundation or early development of many new religious movements: the outstanding example was Joanna Southcott, a domestic servant from Exeter, whose prophecies concerning the imminent millennium won her a nation-wide following during the wars against Napoleon. But those movements which lasted long enough to achieve respectability and to undergo bureaucratisation generally pushed their women members back into the subordinate roles: thus the Primitive Methodists and Bible Christians included women among their travelling preachers in their early years; but by about 1860 it seems that there were only women local preachers, and even they were denied some of the powers held by their male colleagues.[6] The Quakers, who actually had more women than men among their recognised ministers in the earlier nineteenth century, effectively treated organisational matters as a male preserve until the 1890s;[7] at the present day they are probably the only Christian denomination within which there is equality of power between men and women. So most churches have during this period had a male leadership and a mainly female rank and file.

The relationship between class and religion in nineteenth- and twentieth-century Europe has been investigated many times, and some of the more important factors have become well established; but the differences between the characteristic religious outlook of men and women during the same period have only been mentioned in passing. When, for instance, Marrus refers to a 'universal' 'feminisation' of religion in the nineteenth century, this is largely guess-work, as the evidence of the nineteenth century is very scattered, and that for the eighteenth century hardly seems to have been considered.[8] Marrus gives one specific instance in which there is clear evidence of change in this period: the reduced male participation in many local pilgrimages in France. Obelkevich notes another in rural England: the tendency for mainly female choirs to replace male church orchestras. He also suggests that the predominance of women in nineteenth-century rural congregations was an aspect of the decline of community: 'In so far as church attendance had been regarded as a public duty in the traditional society, it appears to have been principally a duty of the husband, as representative of his family and household. When the rise of classes made communal obligations obsolete, religious practice became a matter of individual decision, and women were now free to play a more active role.' At present this is a convincing guess rather than proven fact. But there is evidence that precisely this was happening in rural Germany in the late nineteenth century. In many Protestant peasant areas the custom seems to have been for individuals to attend church as 'representatives' of their farmhouse, and for a different individual to go each week. In the more traditional peasant parishes the result in the 1890s was a fairly even balance between men and women in the congregation. But where, as was generally happening at this time, the custom was breaking down, the proportion of women rose above 60 per cent or even above 70 per cent.[9]

But granted that where church-going ceased to be a legal or a social obligation, it was usually women who kept it up, and men who dropped it, no-one has provided any very satisfactory explanation of why in nineteenth- and twentieth-century Europe such a marked difference should generally have existed. According to the present evidence the tendency for women to be more involved than men in the church applies both to towns and to rural areas, to Catholic and to Protestant countries, to the working class and to the middle class. A starting-point for any investigation must be the recognition that male domination placed strict limits on the areas of activity open to women, and the forms of behaviour by women that were socially acceptable. A second basic point is the general existence of distinctive male and female sub-cultures, with their own rituals, values, *esprit de corps*. Three possible ways of approaching the problem are to focus on the female world and the distinctive experiences of women; to focus on the male world, and the ways in which its concerns and mores came into conflict with those of the church; and to look at the social functions of sharply differentiated sex-roles.

The general tendency of economic change in the nineteenth century was to sharpen the distinction between the economic roles of men and women, and it is sometimes suggested that this sharpened the antagonisms between the sexes, and made for a clearer distinction between male and female worlds. Where factory production replaced the domestic system, men and women, instead of working side by side, worked in different areas of the factory, or in many cases the men went out to work, while the women stayed at home. Wives who had often shared the management of the family business, had no part in running the giant limited company. The wives of ambitious farmers 'abandoned' as Obelkevich puts it, 'the dairy for the parlour, now adorned with a piano'.[10] At first sight this increasingly sharp demarcation between the working lives of men and women provides a promising explanation for the apparent separation of their religious lives. However, direct co-operation between the members of the family in production was usually organised on a basis of a clear differentiation between the tasks characteristically allotted to men and women, adults and children, and does not seem in practice to have precluded the development of male and female sub-cultures. The fact that close co-operation in economic matters could go together with a complete separation of leisure is well illustrated by Le Play's monograph of the 1850s on a small farming family in a wine-growing area of south-western France. Here husband and wife worked together on their own vines, and while the husband was labouring for neighbouring proprietors, the wife grew vegetables, looked after the cow, and took its milk to sell in the town. The husband spent his Sunday drinking, playing cards and denouncing the rich in the bar, while the wife had her chief recreation – apart from twice yearly visits to the fair – in chatting with neighbours while mending linen and clothing. 'When the pig has been killed, relatives and friends are invited in to dinner; the members of the same family hardly see one another except on these occasions.'[11] Conversely in social milieux where it was axiomatic in the nineteenth century that managing a household and bringing up children were the only forms of work appropriate for married women, there was a tendency for an intense family life to develop with very close relationships between spouses and between parents and children.

In the family described by Le Play neither husband nor wife ever went to church; but in other respects the wife would have had much in common with the many poor women in nineteenth-century Europe who found in their hours spent at church almost their only release from household drudgery. In Catholic parishes a host of confraternities, catering for both the spiritual and the social needs of their members, made an important contribution to their often meagre recreational life, as well as giving them a feeling of power and usefulness that extended beyond the home. In Protestant churches, women could act as Sunday School teachers, class leaders, and sometimes local preachers, or join a variety of sisterhoods or mothers' meetings, or else mixed-sex organisations for prayer, bible study, education or sociability. The church was also an important charitable resource: their husbands could afford to scoff, but they had to find ways of clothing the children through the winter and of feeding them when there was little work to be had; regular attendance at church, or membership of a church organisation, might qualify them for help from the St. Vincent de Paul Society, or the church's poor fund, or some wealthy individual in the congregation. A republican weaver, who tried to analyse the hold which the church had on the working-class women of Lyon in the 1850s, found that the church provided above all two things: charity and sociability. And many of these women 'preferred the church that helped them to live and raise their families to their own husbands'.[12]

Meanwhile bourgeois women, who had servants to do all the manual labour in the house, were under pressure to remain at home and act the part of the most beautiful, fragile and expensive of their husband's possessions. The church was about the one place where jealous husbands could almost feel that their wives were safe – though the alleged talents of Catholic priests in seduction caused some anxieties. Church-sponsored organisations were one sphere of public activity from which women were not excluded, and where they could enjoy some degree of status independent of their husbands. So, for instance, we find the proverbially Catholic bourgeois women of Lille playing a progressively smaller part in the economic life of the city during the nineteenth century, but an increasingly important role in charitable activity, including the management of homes for working mothers, crèches, girls' clubs, and a wide range of institutions intended for the benefit of their husbands' employees. The other characteristic sphere of activity of Lille's female élite was prayer: the city abounded with organisations designed to further Catholic or conservative causes, or to secure the physical and spiritual well-being of its people by means of prayer. Incidentally, these were also means of strengthening the ties which bound together the women of the bourgeoisie, emphasising their common identity and values. One such group, the sodality formed by the alumnae of Sacré-Coeur school, an élite *pensionnat* established in the 1840s, believed that their prayers had saved Lille from enemy occupation and civil war in 1870–1, and a chapel built in thanksgiving subsequently became a site of pilgrimage.

Furthermore, many of the characteristic concerns of the churches and the values which they fostered accorded well with the concerns and situation of women. The preoccupation of most branches of nineteenth- and early twentieth-century Christianity with questions of individual morality was quite relevant to the situation of most women, living as they did in a world of face to face contacts, in which personal relationships with neighbours, shopkeepers, children, husbands, were of far more immediate significance than, for instance, the relationship between workers and employers. As one example, Robert Moore, shows the relevance of Methodism to the problems faced by miners' wives in bringing up their children and maintaining their homes according to their standards of decency on incomes that left no margins:

The women had an immediate interest in the behaviour of their menfolk. A drunken, gambling father meant an ill-clad family, no new furniture, and growing debt at the store. It is reported that during missions women had been seen running down the street, still wearing aprons, crying with joy, when hearing of their husband's conversion. Others attended chapel 'to keep their husbands up to the mark'.[13]

In this area of individual morality, church teaching offered the harassed housewife practical answers with tangible results. In their anxiety for the physical and spiritual welfare of their children mothers were to a large degree faced with the humanly uncontrollable, and here prayer often came to seem a vital resource. In nineteenth-century Lille many of the élite belonged to the Archconfraternity of Christian Mothers, founded in 1846 by the wife of a high official after she heard an acquaintance 'weep bitter tears over the spiritual death of her son'. The purpose of the organisation was prayer for the children of members. When a member's children recovered, apparently miraculously, from illness, she would attribute the result to the intercession of the Virgin; when the children died such organisations could at least offer sympathetic friends and the comfort of believing that the death was not a meaningless accident, but part of God's plan. And if the death of children is now an exceptional tragedy, rather than part of the normal experience of most mothers, new circumstances have created new causes for anxieties that no rational means can hold at bay: in the 1960s Portuguese pilgrimage sites were thronged not only with the usual crowds of invalids, but with mothers praying for their sons' safe return from the colonial wars in Africa.

Men, on the other hand, were much less likely to go to church to meet their friends, as they had so many alternatives. For working-class men the towns offered a plethora of benefit societies and drinking places, and although alternatives to the church were fewer in the countryside, there were in the eighteenth and nineteenth century plenty of rural priests who regarded the inn-keeper as their most dangerous rival.

Moreover, many of the characteristic activities of men in their free hours brought them directly into conflict with church morality. One example of this has received a lot of attention from French historians: the widespread practice of *coitus interruptus* by land-hungry French peasants during the nineteenth century brought men specifically into conflict with their priests, as according to the confession manuals the man was regarded as responsible for this practice and required to confess it, while the woman was regarded as a passive victim. In 1842 the bishop of Le Mans claimed that men in his diocese were failing to confess for fear of being grilled about their sex lives, and similar comments were made by a good many other priests at various times in the century, though it must be admitted that French priests had a tendency to become obsessed with 'onanism', which they used as a scapegoat onto which responsibility for almost any undesirable development could be pinned.[14]

More generally men tended to claim for themselves a freedom in such matters as gambling, heavy drinking and promiscuous sex that they denied to their wives and daughters. At all social levels in nineteenth-century Europe these were among the hallmarks of the male sub-culture. The most obvious example of this was the huge prostitution industry, the subject in the nineteenth century of a vast, but, in the nature of things unreliable literature. Zeldin claims that even in the 1960s a quarter of the adult male population of Paris visited brothels.[15]

There were also respects in which church teaching was less relevant to men than to women. If the stress of the clergy on issues of individual morality brought them into touch with the basic concerns of women, and the solutions that they offered often seemed practical, the church had much less to say to a world focussed on economic conflict, in which one party was guided by a faith in the market that found its ultimate expression in Social Darwinism, and the other party was increasingly learning to think in terms of the inevitable war between classes. If some of those involved in industry continued to connect their religion and their work – for instance paternalistic employers and some craftsmen – the logic of economic development was against them in the nineteenth century, as ever-larger firms took on an impersonal, bureaucratic character and human values got lost in the violence of the war between capital and labour. Churchmen accustomed to acting as arbiters in a society where some degree of consensus as to basic values existed, found that in a polarised society the language of consensus and compromise, with which alone they felt at ease, now angered one side and bored the other.

Differences of religious conviction and practice between the sexes could certainly be a source of tension between them. The records of the popular societies during the revolutionary dechristianisation in France are full of criticism for the female members because of their devotion to their churches and priests. Anti-clerical husbands were also jealous of the clergy because of this influence on their wives, and the benefits they were supposed to draw from it. In the 1960s it was still claimed that southern Portuguese peasants preferred to have a priest with a regular mistress, as he was thought less likely to make advances to their wives. On the other hand there were certainly many devout women who were very unhappy on account of the irreligion of their husbands. But the clear differentiation of sex-roles had its advantages in religion as in other areas. The numerous anthropological studies of the concepts of 'honour' and 'shame' in Mediterranean communities may be relevant here. These show that whereas family honour is dependent on the behaviour both of their men and their women, different qualities are demanded of the two sexes. For men the essential is to 'have *cojones*' (testicles). As Pitt-Rivers puts it: 'The quintessence of manliness is fearlessness, readiness to defend one's own pride and that of one's family. It is ascribed to a physical origin, and the idiom in which it is expressed is frankly physiological. To be masculine is to have *cojones*.' For women, however, the essential is *vergüenza* (modesty). Thus a division of labour exists within the household, and is enforced by public opinion, that ensures that men perform the dirty work of engaging in feuds with neighbours, defending the honour of daughters from would-be seducers, and generally furthering the interests of the family in a competitive environment, while women provide a reasonably attractive home in which men rest from the violent world outside, and children can grow up in an atmosphere of relative peace and love. The required female virtues are reinforced at church, and church-going is accordingly considered an appropriate and becoming activity for a woman. On the other hand the values inculcated there accord ill with the required male aggression and refusal to forgive.[16]

This situation would seem most likely to arise where conflicts of economic interest are frequent, work outside the household is mainly a male preserve and strong community controls limit individual freedom of action. It has been most fully studied in Mediterranean peasant communities, but it may equally have applied in many nineteenth-century bourgeois families. As a French doctor wrote in a guide to *The Health of Married People*, published in the 1860s: 'Happiness in marriage is not possible unless each keeps perfectly within his role and confines himself to the virutes of his sex, without encroaching on the prerogatives of the opposite sex.' The husband's function was 'to represent the family or to direct it in its relations with the outside world and to ensure its preservation and development. The wife, so well endowed with grace, intuition, and a ready emotional sympathy, has as her mission to preside over the internal life of the house, whose well-being she ensures by her knowledge of domestic details.' Some of the religious corollaries of this demarcation of spheres of action are implied in the claim of a French woman writer in 1860 that women went to their priest to confess because they could not do it to their stiff and distant husbands, and in the comment that, in early twentieth-century France, men who never went to mass 'took a certain pride in the fact that their wives practised religion and that their children took their first communion and they almost always insisted that their children were baptised'.[17]

3 Three Kinds of Religion

I

In the polarised societies of the nineteenth century and the first half of the twentieth, sectarianism provided for large numbers of people the strongest basis for their social identity. This chapter will look at three types of religious movement which flourished in this period of widespread revolt against the *ancien régime* and the state churches. Two of these – the Protestant sect and the religion of humanity – can be seen as varying forms of emancipation from the old order. The third, Ultramontane Catholicism, was the most effective of the means devised by the older churches to broaden their popular appeal and strengthen their defences against these hostile forces. All of these movements made absolute claims for themselves; they combined aggressive evangelism with the attempt to mark out sharp and clear boundaries between their own community and the world beyond. This was the age of the self-built ideological ghettos – Catholic, Protestant, liberal, socialist. These ideological communities, sometimes a nineteenth-century creation, sometimes built upon older foundations, were often able to maintain over several generations a network of institutions, and a body of collective memories, sacred rites, battle songs, devotions to legendary heroes. As the religious unity of west-European societies broke down, each of the movements which challenged the authority of the state churches tried to impose within its own sphere of influence the totalitarian controls that the state churches had once exercised, and aspired ultimately to provide bonds of unity for whole societies.

II

The end of the eighteenth century and the first half of the nineteenth saw the rise in most parts of Europe of a popular Protestantism that spread through open-air evangelism. The great appeal of this form of Christianity to many peasants, farm labourers, fishermen, miners, craftsmen, and industrial workers lay in its combination of the disciplines of a new morality, some of the magic of the older folk religions, and a gripping emotionalism.

In England, the Methodist movement, which had been growing gradually since Wesley began field-preaching in 1739, took off in the years immediately after his death in 1791. From 57,000 members in 1791 it rose to 92,000 in 1801, 143,000 in 1811, and 489,000 in 1850. In west Cornwall, Methodism's greatest stronghold, 1764 had initiated a century of recurrent revivals, reaching a high point in the 'great revival' of 1814. In Wales the great expansion of Nonconformity began around 1800, and in Scotland the revival of 1799 in Perthshire initiated the religious awakening that would make the Highlands the greatest stronghold of the Free Kirk. In 1796 the Lutheran lay evangelist, Hauge, began his travelling ministry in Norway, which earned him many years in prison, but initiated a period of recurrent revival in the Scandinavian countries, both inside and outside the state churches, that came to an end about 1870. The same period saw the evangelical *Réveil* movement challenge the previously dominant rationalist theology of the French Protestant churches.

All of these movements reasserted the doctrines of the Reformation: the Bible as the unique Word of God, the utter sinfulness of the natural man, the possibility of redemption through God's grace, justification by faith alone. They emphasised that becoming a Christian required an experience of conversion, in which the sinner knew God's forgiveness and was born again. In these years this was often a mass experience, as many people were converted at meetings held expressly for the purpose of 'winning souls' during periods of general 'revival'. These movements continued to grow for most of the century. One essential reason was that they offered the craftsman and the peasant the chance of interpreting the Bible for themselves, unhindered by an educated clergy or by persons of higher status. In their chapels a poor man (and sometimes a poor woman) could become a preacher, class leader, Sunday School teacher.

When in 1863 Abraham Kuyper, freshly graduated from Leiden took up his first charge as minister of the state church in rural Gelderland, he found himself boycotted by a group of malcontents led by a miller's daughter, Pietje Baltus, who accused him of betraying the Reformed Confessions and not teaching 'sovereign grace'.[1] John Galt's novel of 1821, *The Annals of the Parish*, which took the form of the memoirs of the minister of an Ayrshire parish, began with the new minister arriving at the door of the church to find it nailed up by hostile parishioners, with the result that he had to climb in through the window; when at last the ceremony got under way it was interrupted by a weaver called Thomas Thorl, who got up to tell the minister he was 'a thief and a robber'. Galt's hero eventually won Thorl over, and Pietje Baltus won Kuyper over to her traditional Calvinism – with the result that he eventually led an 'orthodox' secession from the state church, and as leader of the ultra-Calvinist Anti-Revolutionary Party became the Dutch Prime Minister. In the early years of the nineteenth century the villages of northern Europe were full of weavers and millers' daughters, many of them beneficiaries of the superior systems of parish schools established in Calvinist and Lutheran countries, who thought that they had as much right as the minister to interpret the Bible, who objected to the powers of the gentry in such matters as church patronage, and who were prepared to break away from the state church if it did not provide them with preaching that was to their taste. Though the minister and malcontent sometimes found common ground, as in the two episodes mentioned, there were also many cases like that on the Isle of Lewis in 1823 where a group of evangelicals jumped up during the sermon at the parish church to object to the doctrines being expounded from the pulpit: when the objectors refused to sit down, they were dragged from the church, and when they went on to attempt to drown the preacher's voice by singing outside, five of them were arrested and spent a month in jail – a punishment that did nothing to halt a process that would culminate at the Disruption of 1843 with only 2 per cent of the island's population remaining within the established church.

The appeal of these movements was essentially to the common people, though not necessarily to the poorest among them. According to A.D. Gilbert's analysis of baptismal and burial registers, English Methodism in the early nineteenth century was dominated by artisans, but labourers, on the other hand, were under-represented.[2] In some parts of Wales Nonconformity seems to have embraced all sections of the population below the level of the gentry or large employers. In the Scottish cities the appeal of the Free Church seems to have been mainly to newly rich members of the middle class, but in the Highlands it embraced the mass of crofters, though again artisans seem to have been prominent in the leadership. In Sweden smallholders were said to be the strongest supporters of the free church movement, and most accounts of the Calvinist secessions in the Netherlands stress the low social status of the dissidents. It was part of the strength of the leaders of these movements that they moved in the same thought world as that of the smallholders and weavers who listened to them, and they spoke the same language – the latter point being especially important in such places as Wales, the Scottish Highlands, Friesland or Lappland, where ignorance of the national language was one of the essential barriers between the common people and the clergy of the established church. They offered an exciting religion, in which experience counted for more than learning. Local preachers and itinerant evangelists deliberately whipped their audiences up to a frenzy of excitement in which they longed for the relief of conversion experience. In the earlier stages of a revival meeting there were sounds of groaning from men and women who had for the first time become fully conscious of the fact that they were sinners and needed God's forgiveness. As the meeting approached its climax there would be an unbearable tension. And then as the first converts 'found liberty' they would begin to shout or jump with joy.

Conversions won in such conditions were often short-lived. But for those who stayed, religion continued to be exciting, though also extremely demanding. In the early years of Primitive Methodism, for instance, a body of 'saints' would walk out to an unevangelised village, and start processing through the streets singing hymns, until an audience gathered and the preaching could begin – and sometimes the basis for a new congregation was laid, though they often had to run a gauntlet of ridicule or violence before they made any impression. After many days of hard and often meagrely rewarded labour they could bring back some of the euphoria of their own conversion, and bask in the sense of solidarity with thousands of like-minded souls by singing their favourite hymns and enjoying the oratory at one of their huge camp-meetings, often held high up on the Pennine moors.

The popular evangelicalism of these years also filled some of the gap between official religion and folk religion that had widened at the Reformation, and become a chasm in the eighteenth century as an increasingly rational-minded clergy had lost touch with the forms of thought of the superstitious masses. The popular preachers of these years, however, while they were for the most part ardent exponents of Reformation Protestantism, also lived in the world of dreams, visions, exorcisms, divination, witchcraft, which played such a large part in the lives of the people they preached to. It has been argued that the triumph of Methodism in Cornwall owed much to the congruence between Methodist beliefs and the various superstitions that played a big part in the lives of the miners and fishermen: 'Methodism did not so much displace the folk beliefs as translate them into a religious idiom.' Both belief-systems assumed the continual intervention by supernatural powers in day to day life, and saw the hand whether of witches and fairies, of God or the devil, in every unexpected event. Both offered propitiatory rituals which offered hope of safety in a life where death was always very close.[3] Methodist preachers were also credited with the same powers that were commonly attributed to wise men – or to Catholic priests. In south Lancashire they called in a Wesleyan local preacher to cast out a sofa-raising boggart; in Devon Bible Christian preachers could trace lost pigs. And in the Scottish Highlands, 'The Men', as the local evangelical leaders were called, often claimed to have second sight; as James Hunter puts it, they combined 'a harsh and pristine puritanism with a transcendental mysticism that had less to do with nineteenth-century Protestantism than with an older faith. Visions of heaven and hell, prophetic utterance, intensely personal conflicts with the devil and his angels: these were integral to their creed and a common part of their experience; while in their preaching homely illustration was combined with mysticism and allegory.'[4]

Yet if the 'transcendental mysticism' was essential to the initial impact of these movements, in the longer term the 'harsh and pristine puritanism' was perhaps even more important. It was certainly in terms of the putting off of an old way of life and the putting on of the new that conversion was often presented. Robert Colls comments that conversion 'resulted in the convert transforming his self-image and therefore his habits'; he quotes the Primitive Methodist John Wilson, leader of the Durham Miners' Association in the later nineteenth century, to the effect that his conversion led him to give up drinking and gambling, and made him see his life in new terms as a gift and something to be stewarded.[5] Robert Moore, referring to the Durham mining villages around the time of Wilson's ascendancy, quotes a favourite Methodist story of a recent convert who was grilled by his workmates about miracles and replied by asking the men 'if they remembered his family and the state of his home six months ago; and did they know what it was like now? Well if Jesus could turn beer into clothes for his children and furniture for his house, would He not be able to turn water into wine?'[6] In Cornwall, earlier in the century, Methodists would go to fairs in order to preach against the activities they saw there. Evangelical propaganda attacked all those forms of behaviour that appeared idle, irresponsible, undisciplined, wasteful.

Above all, nineteenth-century popular Protestantism found in alcohol the great symbol of everything it opposed. Before about 1830 evangelicals had been content to attack drunkenness and 'wasting time' in drinking places; drinking in moderate quantities, and for the purpose of refreshment, was accepted as normal. But from the early 1830s teetotal societies were being formed, mainly in Britain, Ireland and Scandinavia, and by the end of the century teetotalism had become so much a shibboleth that total abstinence appeared to be the basic tenet of British Nonconformity and Scandinavian Pietism. The basic reason for this, perhaps, was that drink provided a tangible, universally recognisable target (much better than 'sin'), and the drunkard personified everything the evangelicals would sweep away – as useful as the stereotype of the idle aristocrat, bloated capitalist, or tyrannical priest for other reformers. Far more effective than any generalised call to repentance was the banner carried through the streets of Camborne by the local teetotallers at their annual fair in 1849: '8,000 drunkards go to hell every year.'

Drink, or at least the public house, was also a formidable rival. Most accounts of working-class life in nineteenth-century Europe emphasise the great importance of drinking places in male leisure, and reformers of most hues complained that their potential audiences were relaxing in a pub when they could have been attending their meetings. A connected point was that as public drinking places were mainly parts of male sub-cultures they were suspect to those reformers who saw the good life as something that was lived as a family. Drink was also condemned for its associations – cruel sports, gambling, sexual promiscuity. But teetotalism had in the 1830s and 1840s an appeal that extended beyond the bounds of the Protestant sects to include radicals and secularists. There were many Chartists who saw drink as one of the principal means by which the people were enslaved by their rulers; Henry Vincent, the leader of the Teetotal Chartists, looked forward to a time when, with the abandonment of drink, 'the people will be too proud to wear the degraded livery of a policeman, or to enlist as soldiers, to murder at the bidding of an aristocrat their unoffending brothers for a shilling a day'. Political radicals and evangelical sectarians shared a hostility to most of the traditional forms of popular amusement, which they regarded as crude and degrading; instead they stressed the virtues of knowledge, industry, and a rational, calculating mentality. Typical was the claim of a Methodist miner that his religion made him an autonomous individual, rather than 'a mere machine for hewing coals'.[7] Both groups saw in alcohol, the clouder of the mind, and the basis for a culture of easy-going good fellowship, a prime obstacle to the 'improvement' for which they hoped. 'Teetotalism,' comments Brian Harrison, in writing of the Preston Pioneers, 'was a convenient way of combining political and religious radicalism'. These pioneers were drawn from the working class or lower middle class, and combined religious Nonconformity with radical Liberalism. A typical combination of interests was that of Joseph Livesey, a weaver turned cheesemonger, who was an enthusiast for education, and one of the founders of the mechanics' institute in Preston, an advocate of universal suffrage and the ballot, and a champion of hand-loom weavers, an enemy of cruel sports, the established church, and the New Poor Law.[8]

Of course in some instances evangelical sectarians and political radicals were the same people: for instance the parallel between the demands for democracy in the church and in society at large is particularly evident in the history of the Methodist secessions in the early decades of the nineteenth century. In other instances the two groups were at one another's throats, the more so, perhaps, because both looked to much the same constituency. This considerable overlap in ideas, membership, and overall social constituency suggests that at least in the early nineteenth century some of the same causes lay behind both movements. Of these one of the most important was the demand of the ordinary worker for dignity and self-respect, at a time when paternalism was breaking down, and a competitive bourgeois society assessed worth in terms of achievement. Typical of this concern was the promise made by Joseph Arch, Primitive Methodist preacher and leader of the farm labourers' union: 'The day is not far distant when you will no longer be called joskins and clodhoppers, but acknowledged as free citizens of the land.'[9] And the first step towards emancipation, for religious and secular reformers alike, seemed to be the abandonment of those customs which had merited such contempt. For groups of rural labourers, accustomed to being treated like children, the disciplined life-style and the puritanism associated with Nonconformity and temperance were ways of asserting that they were adults, and intended to claim the rights and responsibilities of adults – indeed an exaggerated puritanism might be a way of claiming moral superiority over social 'superiors'. There was also an immense optimism lying behind the movement for moral reform: education, self-discipline, hard work and the abolition of privilege were the keys to a prosperous, humane and egalitarian society. Each group had its own special hopes, but it was common ground between many varieties of Protestant sectarian and secular radical that the period since the Revolution in France and the beginnings of industrialisation in Britain marked a new era of vast potential. As the English Baptist leader, Robert Hall, put it:

We see whole kingdoms . . . start from their slumber, the dignity of man rising up from depression, and tyrants trembling on their throne . . . We need not wonder if among events so extraordinary the human character itself should appear to be altering and improving apace . . . Man seems to be becoming more erect and independent. He leans more on himself, less on his fellow creatures. He begins to feel a consciousness in a higher degree of personal dignity and is less enamoured of artificial distinctions. There is some hope of our beholding that simplicity and energy of character which marks his natural state blended with the humanity, the elegance and improvement of polished society.[10]

But in practice one of the main consequences of these evangelical movements was to produce a moral cleavage within many communities. In the later nineteenth century there was said to be a fundamental division in rural Wales between 'the people of the religious meeting' and 'the people of the tavern'. The same point, slightly more nuanced, is made in an account of the area around Merthyr Tydfil in the nineteenth century:

A person could be a chapel-goer, less frequently a church-goer, or, at the other extreme, the public house was his only social centre. . . . Between the two extremes of chapel and public house were the clubs, or benefit-societies which met in the latter. . . . It was from this class of benefit-society men that Nonconformity drew its largest number of adherents (*y gwrandawyr*) who formed an outer shell to Nonconformity statistically far more imposing than the membership itself.[11]

So besides the conflict of classes, and the sectarian conflicts with which nineteenth-century Europe abounded, there was also in many places a recurrent conflict within the same social milieu between the adherents of opposing moralities. In Britain a characteristic form of this conflict was the chapel/pub dichotomy, though there were of course 'respectables' who were secularists or who were adherents of the established churches. The division was probably clearest in small communities, where a relatively clear polarisation might develop – so that, for instance, the future Labour M.P. Harry Snell, returning in the 1880s from Nottingham to his native village would find that the young men were all either 'chapel' or 'pub', and that he as a teetotal secularist belonged to neither.[12] In a town or city a more complex pattern of oppositions could develop, like that in Banbury in the mid-nineteenth century, where Harrison and Trinder distinguish two elements within the 'respectable' working class, one of which favoured a moderate radicalism, and gave priority to temperance and self-help; the other being also teetotal, and including both Nonconformists and secularists, but giving priority to class issues.[13] In those smaller village communities complex and ambivalent relationships between 'chapel' and 'pub' could develop. Naturally there was some movement from one world to the other; and within families some divided allegiance. Also parents who never went near the chapel themselves in normal circumstances, sent their children to Sunday School, and themselves turned up for the Sunday School anniversary. Furthermore in the nineteenth century and early twentieth century it was often from the chapel that working-class leadership was drawn. Men who in other circumstances treated the chapel-goers with irony might still prefer a chapel-goer as treasurer of union branch funds, and would respond eagerly to the biblical rhetoric in which a Tommy Hepburn or a Joseph Arch argued their case. On the other hand no mercy was shown to a saint who was shown to be a hypocrite. In the Somerset village of Pilton in 1909 a middle-aged married Methodist was having an affair with a teenage girl, so a group of roughs decided over their beer one evening to light a bonfire in the field behind his cottage and burn him in effigy; he left the village the next morning. If he had made no special claim to virtue they would not have bothered, but they felt he was trying to have his his cake and eat it, and an example would have to be made of him.[14]

III

The cult of reason in 1793 was the first of many attempts to build a new religion of humanity on the ruins of the old supernaturalism. In practice, though not in original intention, Freemasonry was to be among the most important of these. While in Britain it had no special religious or political significance, in many Catholic countries it became 'the International of the revolutionary middle classes in their struggle against feudal and religious institutions'.[15] Though the masons' religious doctrine had little specific content, their emphasis on toleration and on morality as the essence of good living, was in itself an implicit challenge to the increasingly dogmatic and exclusive Catholicism of the nineteenth century. Throughout the period of the Third Republic in France the influence of the Masonic lodges was quite disproportionate to their small membership. From Gambetta to Léon Blum probably a majority of the leading figures on the Left were masons. Links were closest with the Radicals; but they included many Socialists too. The lodges provided a pressure group on behalf of republican causes; a rival to the church in its charitable work, and even in its rituals and rites of passage; and a means by which republican politicians could make contacts and establish their credentials. In so far as these middle-class anti-clericals had a unifying ideology it was positivism. The prophet of this creed was Auguste Comte (1798–1857) who eventually developed it into a full-scale Religion of Humanity – so ecclesiastical in form that British critics called it 'Catholicism minus Christianity'. But there were many positivists who, without adopting the ritualised form, were inspired by the idea that the progress of humanity gave larger significance to the short life of the individual, that altruism provided a higher motive than the Christian's hope of individual salvation, that science offered men a solid understanding of their natural and social environment; the puritanical ethics of the new creed also seemed to refute the Catholic accusation that to dispense with a supernatural God was to open the floodgates of hedonistic individualism.

In the late 1870s, with the republican takeover of national power and of numerous local authorities, these principles could be imparted to the population at large through the schools. In the 1880s many schools were forcibly laicised (which sometimes meant that soldiers were brought in to eject the monks and nuns, while parents hurled insults or missiles at the agents of the law); meanwhile clergymen were deprived of all influence over state education, and religious teaching in state schools was stopped. The primary school teachers were then sent forth, as the son of one of them put it, 'to fight the atrocious trinity of royalism, church and alcohol'. That first generation of lay primary school teachers is now remembered (at least by those in their own tradition) as saints.[16] Like the priests they were representative individuals, personifying something far greater than themselves, and so constrained to superhuman standards of rectitude and propriety. Neither peasant nor bourgeois, they were required to know their people intimately yet never be one of them; they were lonely, potential victims of all the savage innuendoes of village gossip. The one person whose situation was similar to their own was their bitter rival, the parish priest.

Positivism had a great influence on the élite of the French Third Republic, and indeed on the liberal middle class of Spain and Latin America. But the greatest of the nineteenth-century's religions of humanity, and the only one with a mass appeal, was socialism.

Religious language and analogies were continually used by the pioneers of socialism. It is impossible to understand the appeal that the movement had – or the conflicts that often ensued between socialists and churchmen – without recognising that socialist parties were far more than pressure groups on behalf of the working class. Like the sansculottes of 1793 they claimed to offer a formula for the total regeneration of society. Like the Christian churches they claimed to preach all that was necessary to salvation. And like evangelicals who preached 'salvation' and nothing else, they believed that socialism held the key to human emancipation, and all else would follow from it. It was this exclusiveness in the claims made by each, more than disagreement on any specific point, that tended to bring Christians and socialists into conflict. The point was clear to Paul Göhre, a pastor who later became a Social Democrat, and who concluded from his experiences in Chemnitz in the 1890s that 'the social democracy of today is not merely a political party, or a new system of economics, or even both of these put together; it is a new conception of the world and of life'.[17] In Germany the first socialist parties were formed in the 1860s, and in 1875 they united to form the SAPD (later SPD), which soon won a large working-class following, and remained the largest and most influential of Europe's socialist parties until upstaged by the Bolsheviks. A socialist party was formed in Austria in 1874, in France in 1879, and in most other parts of Europe in the 1880s. They varied greatly in strength, and in some countries, notably Britain and France, there were several competing socialist parties. In others, notably Spain, 'libertarian social-ism' (anarchism) was an attractive alternative to the Marxist or reformist varieties. Enthusiasm and levels of commitment have fluctuated. But socialism has remained to this day the strongest ideological influence on the European working class.

Wherever socialism established itself in the late nineteenth century it tended to form a network of supporting institutions, rather similar to that which the Catholic church used to strengthen the bonds between the faithful and to preserve them from the contamination of 'the world'. This tendency was very fully developed in pre-1914 Germany. In Chemnitz in the 1890s, for instance, Göhre noted that although the number of committed and informed socialists was small, a much higher proportion of the working class was partly involved in the socialist sub-culture, through attending the nightly debates and lectures in party clubs, or the Sunday festivals for socialist families, reading party newspapers, and belonging to one or other of the numerous organisations which, from crèche to crematorium, enabled the comrade to live and die in a socialist environment.[18] In the suburb where Göhre lived, over 80 per cent of the voters chose the SPD. Not that active socialism was to be undertaken lightly in Imperial Germany: many party militants had spells in prison both during and after the anti-socialist law of 1878–90; others lost their jobs. Some of the next generation would die for their socialism in the abortive communist risings of 1919 and after, or in Hitler's concentration camps.

The immense appeal of socialism to the European working class in the last quarter of the nineteenth century and the first half of the twentieth had several dimensions, of which the poverty of most workers, and the obvious urgency of the redistribution of wealth, was only one. Equally important was the fact that capitalist society denied the mass of people dignity, or power over their lives. As Göhre put it, the labour question was not just a stomach question: it was also a demand for 'respect and recognition, for a greater social equality'. He gave as an instance the resentment caused by the lengthy book of rules that was handed to everyone who came to work in a Chemnitz engineering works: 'They are plainly the product of the management, fashioned solely according to its idea of its own selfish interests . . . Their existence and validity proclaim in every case of importance, the complete and unappealable subjection of the working class . . .'.[19]

Socialism also satisfied the worker's thirst for knowledge, and for an understanding of society and his own place in it. A study of Viennese working-class life in the 1890s stressed the big role of the workers' educational associations organised by the Social Democrats,[20] and both in Austria and Germany numerous 'workers' libraries' were founded around this time. The purpose of socialist education was not only to provide factual information, but to give the workers an alternative framework of understanding to that which they had received at school – a framework that was based on an explicit materialism and naturalism, and on an awareness of the class struggle.

In the face of contempt, and often active persecution, the socialists of Germany anticipated the revolution by forming their own alternative society, which replaced the institutions, ideas, rituals, and ethics of the wider society at every point that this was possible.

IV

The state Protestant churches spent much of the nineteenth century fighting an uphill battle against sectarian forms of Christianity with a much more popular style; by the end of the century all forms of Protestantism were generally losing ground to socialism. The Catholic church, on the other hand was more successful in developing forms of piety that were both popular and orthodox, and in keeping rival ideologies at bay.

In the years after 1815 many of the Catholic clergy developed a full-scale ideology of resistance to 'the modern world'. At the centre this took the form of resounding papal condemnations of liberalism in an encyclical of 1832 and in the Syllabus of Errors (1864), the promulgation in 1854 of the doctrine of the Immaculate Conception of the Virgin Mary, and the declaration of papal infallibility in 1870. At the local level it meant an emphatically supernaturalist Catholicism, dedicated to alliance with what was seen as the faith of the common people against the false hopes of rationalism, scientism and liberalism. Under the French Restoration the bishops had tended to be fairly similar to those of the old regime: men more notable for their aristocratic birth and reactionary politics than their piety; in ecclesiastical politics they were Gallicans, committed to the semi-autonomy of the French church, and owing allegiance to the king rather than the pope. Many of the parish clergy were equally gallican. With the great expansion of the priesthood in the 1820s the new recruits were drawn increasingly from the peasantry. Out of sympathy with their bishops, and after 1830 with the French government, they looked for inspiration 'beyond the mountains' to Rome – thus the name 'Ultramontanism' of the movement that was to dominate nineteenth-century Catholicism. Initially a movement of the lower clergy in France, by the 1850s it was being pursued by many of the bishops as well. In terms of French politics Ultramontanism, after the defeat of Lamennais's radical version of the doctrine, was heavily Legitimist. But the precise political location of the party was a local accident. The essence of their creed was the combination of a highly dogmatic and anti-rationalist theology with a warmly emotional piety, and a preference for life within a Catholic ghetto, where the faith of the masses could be preserved from Protestant or rationalist contamination.

The Ultramontanes took a poor view of unaided human nature. But, with God's help, they believed, all things were possible. They were fervent believers in miracles: miracles of healing, of conversion, of deliverance from plagues, invasions, sudden death – miracles often achieved through the prayers of simple people. In the 1870s a wave of prophecies and of alleged miracles or appearances by Jesus, Mary and the saints hit France in the aftermath of defeat by Prussia, and during the prolonged political crisis that followed the fall of Napoleon III. This trend disturbed some leading Catholics, such as bishop Dupanloup, a moderate conservative, who felt that this sort of thing gave Catholicism a bad name, and put off those republicans who might be prepared to co-operate with the church. However, the Ultramontane journalist, Louis Veuillot, who had a great following among the parish clergy, replied that the immediacy of the supernatural was essential to the church's message, and that the true irrationalists were not those who gave credit to these prophecies and visions, but those who believed in 'the chimeras of the Revolution'.[21]

In this spirit, many French priests, around the middle of the century were attempting to take over local pilgrimages which had previously had little connection with the church, and to give them more orthodox Catholic content. In the early decades of the century many parishes had had no resident priest, and in others clergymen influenced by Jansenism or the Enlightenment had tried to dissociate the church from popular 'superstition'. But by the 1860s, in the model Ultramontane diocese of Arras, the bishop was encouraging his clergy to take an interest in pilgrimages and the cult of saints, and a great many lives of saints were being published. From 1866 the diocese was led by a 'veritable pilgrim bishop'. Much the same was happening in the diocese of Montpellier where, until the 1870s, the bishops had looked somewhat askance at the colourful forms of devotion favoured by the local population: from then on the bishops themselves were at the head of the processions.[22]

Above all the Ultramontanes lent their support to the cult of Mary and to the various national and international pilgrimage sites that became established from the middle of the nineteenth century to the middle of the twentieth following appearances by the Virgin. Most of these appearances took place in remote rural spots; and there were a great many others reported in similar areas that never received episcopal authentication, or became the basis for a cult extending beyond the immediate locality. The most popular of all these new shrines was Lourdes in the French Pyrenees, where the Virgin appeared to the fourteen-year-old Bernadette Soubirous in 1858. Other notable examples include La Salette in the French Alps (1846), Knock in Ireland (1879),

Fatima in Portugal (1917), Banneux in Belgium (1933). The pilgrims who came to ask favours of Mary at the sacred places were drawn from far as well as near, from the cities as well as the villages and hamlets, from a wide range of social classes – according to a French observer of 1873, 'nobles and peasants, workers and soldiers, deputies to the National Assembly, church dignitaries, state officials'.[23]

In times of political crisis these shrines often took on a significance that must have been far from the minds of the individuals whose experiences had laid the basis for the cult. For instance, in the 1870s and 1880s there was a series of big pilgrimages in France that were primarily Legitimist demonstrations, and in 1942 the Petainists staged a 'national youth pilgrimage' to Lourdes. More recently Our Lady of Fatima has been reputed to be the deadliest foe of the Communist party in northern Portugal. More generally the pilgrims came in small groups of ordinary Catholics, many of them hoping to be cured of sickness, or having other private anxieties that needed to be resolved.

Perhaps the most important of the new developments was the great revival of the religious orders, which played a central part in Catholic life during the second half of the nineteenth century and the first half of the twentieth. In France the numbers in religious orders rose from 37,000 to 162,000 between 1851 and 1901 (three-quarters of these being nuns); in Spain there were 15,000 in 1861, 68,000 in 1920 (with a similar ratio of nuns to monks). In the later eighteenth century and the early nineteenth, monks and nuns had seemed to be a dying race: the effects of external attack by secularising governments was reinforced by internal decay. But from the time of Bismarck's *Kulturkampf* to that of the Spanish Second Republic, attacks on the orders were dictated by the fact that they were all too active. The Jesuits were reconstituted in 1814 – and they soon recaptured their old prestige, and (so far as Protestants and anti-papal Catholics were concerned) their old notoriety. A host of new orders were formed during the century, some of which like the Assumptionists (founded in France in 1850) were to rival the Jesuits as exponents of an intransigent Ultramontanism, while others concentrated on less controversial areas of devotion or service. In part the monastic revival represented a return to the religious heroism of the Counter-Reformation period and a reassertion of Tridentine religious ideals: the belief that, as Frances Lannon puts it, in her study of religious communities in Bilbao, 'God was to be found not in the world, but apart from it', and that communities of men and women, who had renounced the pleasures of this life, could provide a bridge between God and the ordinary believer, tied to the workaday secular world with all its temptations and compromises.[24] In strongly Catholic communities the 'fathers' and 'sisters' became familiar and often dearly-loved figures. In an anti-clerical environment like that of the poorer districts of Barcelona they acquired an equally formidable, but much more sinister reputation – for wealth, tyranny and sadism. In the 'tragic week' of July 1909 some eighty religious institutions were set on fire, including those of apparently innocuous nursing orders.

In part the new orders were the Catholic response to new social circumstances, requiring teams of specialists. One example of this was the big role of some orders in establishing Catholic newspapers; another was the formation of orders specialising in foreign missions. But the most important example was the essential part played by the orders in the expansion of education at all levels during the nineteenth century. In Spain, particularly, the orders filled part of the vacuum left by the insufficient number of state schools, and a complete hierarchy of religious schools appeared, ranging from the Jesuit university of Deusto (1886), a training ground for the next generation of industrialists and conservative politicians in northern Spain, to the free schools of the La Salle Brothers.

Since the 1940s members of the religious orders have been in the forefront of the development of a socially radical Catholicism. For instance the Dominicans played a leading part in the French worker-priest movement, and the French provinces of the order were purged after the destruction of the movement by the Vatican in 1954. In the later nineteenth century the orders used their influence in the schools, and in many parishes, to favour Ultramontane religion and right-wing politics. It was, of course, the right-wing politics that worried governments and radical activists. But for many ordinary Catholics the part they played in stimulating the new Ultramontane piety may have been of more direct consequence. In Ireland, for instance, the years from about 1850 to 1875 have been identified as those of a 'devotional revolution', in which the clergy established a dominant influence over the religious life of the people, and patterns of Catholic life were established that have remained up to the present day. The Ultramontane clergy took over and often gave new form to the older folk religion focussed on pilgrimages at specific points of the year, or in times of trouble, and meanwhile imposed on the great majority of Catholics a weekly rhythm of attendance at mass, which was novel for many of them. At the same time they built bigger and more richly decorated churches, made more use of music, incense, banners, processions in their worship; encouraged the use of beads, scapulars, medallions; and introduced cults like that of the Sacred Heart, which gave form to a warm-hearted and sentimental piety – cloying to the Protestant or the more old-fashioned Catholic, but still immensely popular.[25]

V

In spite of their long-term optimism, Catholics, as much as socialists, realised that in the short term the faithful needed to be protected from over-close contact with an unbelieving world, and provided with alternative sources of knowledge, sociability and identity. Ultramontane theology provided the rationale, while Protestant or anti-clerical persecution often provided the occasion for the construction in the second half of the nineteenth century of Catholic ghettos, very similar in form to those which the socialists were constructing around the same time. Where the socialists had their evening classes, the Catholics went one better, establishing their separate system of day schools in all Protestant-dominated countries, and in those predominantly Catholic countries where liberal governments had established secular schools. Like the socialists, Catholics often had their own daily newspapers; in some instances they were able to compete with the most uninhibited sections of the 'yellow press'; *La Croix*, for instance, was one of France's most popular papers in the 1880s and 1890s, specialising in reports of crime, executions and disasters (always interpreted as providential judgements).[26] Especially after *Rerum Novarum*, Leo XIII's encyclical of 1891, which appealed to Catholics to undercut the appeal of socialism by taking the initiative in the fight against bad living and working conditions, priests were forming trade unions and benefit organisations – which won a large following in such areas as Alsace, the Ruhr, Flanders and the southern Netherlands. In Germany, Catholics like socialists expressed their separate identity by adapting Protestant and patriotic songs to deliver a sectarian message: at the annual festivals of the Catholic workers' associations held in the Ruhr in the 1880s they would sing 'I am a Catholic' to the tune of 'I am a Prussian'; meanwhile the socialists sang 'Ein' feste Burg ist unser Bund . . .' (one of at least half a dozen socialist versions of Luther's hymn). Both socialists and Catholics knew how to mix fun with the serious business of demonstrating their strength and tightening the bonds that united the faithful. The German socialists had an alternative calendar, in which festivals commemorating such events as the death of Lassalle replaced the officially recognised patriotic and religious festivities, and these occasions were marked by parades, singing, speeches and beer-drinking. In France in the early twentieth century rival Catholic and republican sports clubs confronted one another in many towns, and there were nation-wide federations of Catholic, socialist and secularist athletic associations.[27] The Catholic equivalent of the socialist festival was the pilgrimage, sometimes organised on a gigantic scale. At Trier, for instance in the autumn of 1891, when the seamless garment of Christ was put on display for the first time in fifty years, it was estimated that a million pilgrims came from all over western Germany – to seek miraculous cures, to savour sermons extolling 'honourable poverty' or denouncing socialism and Protestantism, to admire the huge electric illuminations, and to enjoy the biggest outing of their lives. Sometimes Catholic and socialist displays of strength came into direct opposition, as in October 1903 in Bilbao, where pilgrims en route to the shrine of the Virgin of Begoña clashed with a socialist demonstration and one of the Catholics was killed: this became a legendary incident recalled by Catholic orators for years afterwards.

Both Catholics and socialists tended to view life beyond the ghetto walls in lurid colours, and both camps tended to dissipate much of their energy in conflicts between moderates and intransigents. Pius IX epitomised the position of many Catholic intransigents, when he told a group of French pilgrims in 1871: 'What I fear for you is not that miserable band of Communards (demons escaped from Hell) – but Catholic liberalism. . . . that fatal system that dreams of reconciling two irreconcilables – Church and revolution.'[28] The paranoia of conservative Catholics perhaps reached its most extreme point in Spain. Representative of much Spanish Catholic opinion in the early twentieth century was the *Messenger* of the Apostleship of the Sacred Heart, the country's most widely read religious periodical. In an editorial of 1916 it recalled that: 'We have sounded the alarm against the audacities of socialism, against Protestant propaganda, against the contagions of modernism and recently against the irreligious and anti-patriotic campaign of the liberal press in favour of the Jews.' The paper constantly returned to the fact that Spain had been great when it was truly Catholic and it had declined ever since: by 1922 it was calling for a 'crusade' to make Spain fully Catholic again. Its biggest target of all was the wing of the church that it branded as 'liberal'.[29] Similarly fratricidal strife divided orthodox socialists from revisionists around the turn of the century, and later socialists from communists; but most agreed in regarding non-socialists in terms of a series of hostile stereotypes that hardly helped in the task of winning over such potentially socialist, but in practice largely antagonistic groups as Catholic workers and white collar employees. A good example of this stance would be Robert Tressell's classic novel about Hastings building workers, *The Ragged Trousered Philanthropists* (published in 1914), often cited as 'the book that made me a socialist'. In spite of Tressell's powerful descriptions of poverty, and superb renderings of such episodes as the firm's annual outing, his criticism of 'the system' is made less effective by the crude stereotyping of most of the characters: the two socialists being paragons of all the virtues, while non-socialist workmen are depicted as drunken and stupid; an evangelical among them divides his time between pilfering materials and seducing the wife of a workmate, and employers and foremen are all calculating crooks.

4 The Countryside

I

In 1959 the French rural sociologist Henri Mendras compared the 'dechristianised' country districts, where the priest 'spends his life on the road' visiting the sick, saying mass, co-ordinating the activities of the small numbers of the faithful in half a dozen villages, and exercising no widespread influence in any of them, with those Breton parishes where he 'very largely retains the authority of former years':

He acts as intermediary between his flock and the supernatural; he passes on the wishes of divine authority, and puts them in the right relationship with it at the great moments of their lives. Equally naturally he acts as intermediary and interpreter for his parishioners vis-à-vis secular authority. And this dual role naturally extends into a paternal authority that is widely recognised and which makes him, since the departure of the other *notables*, the real leader of the parish, able to intervene both in the intimacies of family life and in the political concerns of the group.[1]

At the time when Mendras was writing, equally striking contrasts between rural regions of other European countries could have been observed. In Spain and Portugal the devout north was a world apart from the anti-clerical south. In the Netherlands census statements of religious affiliation showed that support for each of the four main groups (Roman Catholic, Dutch Reformed, ultra-Calvinist, and no religion) ranged from under 5 per cent to over 80 per cent according to census district. Elsewhere these regional contrasts were less extreme. The only countries where they had more or less disappeared were the Irish Republic, where the rural population was overwhelmingly made up of practising Catholics, and England, where few people lived in the countryside, and even fewer worked there; but in those English counties which still had a large rural population there was a fairly even pattern of 10–20 per cent church attendance, with the majority of the church-goers being Anglican.

Thus in spite of the revolution in communications and the many changes in agriculture and in rural life, distinctive local traditions still had a large influence on religious life in most parts of Western Europe. In the nineteenth century the localisation of culture was certainly much more general and far-reaching. Although some impoverished regions had a highly developed system of seasonal migration (from the Massif Central to work in the Paris building trades, from the Pyrenees to bring in the grape harvest in coastal Languedoc, for example), many of these migrations did very little to break down the isolation of the homeland, since the migrant workers usually lived and worked together seldom communicating with the surrounding population.[2] For the most part bad roads, mutually incomprehensible languages or patois, illiteracy and poverty, severely limited the contacts between one region and another; and even within such relatively small areas as an English county or a French *département* sharp differences of economy and social structure set off one small area from another, and contrasting local cultures developed. Obelkevich, for instance, in his study of South Lindsey in the mid-nineteenth century divides this area some 40 miles wide and 15 miles deep into 'a well-defined set of eight regions which had their own economic, social, and sometimes religious character', though their average population was less than 10,000 each; on the other hand the people of Lindsey had some sense of common identity *vis-à-vis* the 'yallowbellies' living beyond the river Witham, who spoke a distinct south Lincolnshire dialect. Hilaire, in his study of the Pas-de-Calais during the same period, divides the *département* into nine *pays*, each a 'separate world'.[3] One striking reflection of this localisation of culture was the enormous variety of communal dances, which flourished in France, for instance, until the late nineteenth century; the strength of local identities and the narrowness of horizons also found expression in numerous feuds between the people of neighbouring communities, often breaking out in open violence at fairs or on saints' days. In religious life this localisation was very marked at the beginning of the nineteenth century; by the end of the nineteenth century, contrasts between rural areas remained strong, as each tended to be integrated into mutually antagonistic nationally organised sub-cultures.

One point was general: a supernaturalist view of the world, in which religion and magic were intimately related. The rural population of nineteenth-century Europe lived in a dangerous world in which droughts, hail-storms, crop blights, animal epidemics continually threatened the precarious livelihood of the population, and in which the peasant had few natural means of defending himself against such disasters. Prayers, pilgrimages, spells, rituals of all kinds were called in aid by the individual or by the community as a whole. Belief in the proximity of a world of spirits potent for good or evil, and in the significance of particular times, places, objects, animals as harbingers of good or ill fortune patterned all areas of life. Everywhere the institutions of Christianity were in some measure bound up with this magical world;

but the precise nature of the relationship between magic and the church varied greatly, just as did the specific forms of this magic.

The extreme localisation of many of the forms of religious life and of magic existed for the same reason as the localisation of dance-forms – the fact that each was the product of continuous local development in accordance with local needs by communities of largely illiterate people. Indeed in some respects distinctive local forms were an important part of a communal identity set over against that of neighbouring communities. Thus, for instance, the multitude of local saints in Catholic Europe, many of them unknown outside a particular parish or district – not to mention the necessarily unique holy places (springs, wells, rocks) which were local centres of pilgrimage by anxious individuals throughout the year, and by whole communities on a given day. Cholvy refers to the saints canonised purely by 'the voice of the people', like St. Gent, patron of those suffering from fevers and 'a kind of demi-god for the peasants on the two sides of the Durance', whose hermitage attracted 20,000 visitors in May and September of each year in the 1860s.[4] New saints and accordingly new places of pilgrimage were continually being born, as living men and women won a local reputation for holiness. One such was Jordan Mai, a Dortmund Franciscan, who died in 1922; he was first buried in a city cemetery, but after devotees had taken away most of the earth covering his coffin, his remains were transferred to a Franciscan church, which became a place of pilgrimage.[5] In Protestantism this localisation of religious forms was reflected in the many sects, often inspired by a single leader, and with a highly concentrated following. In England the tensions within the Methodist movement during the first half of the nineteenth century led to a series of locally based secessions from the main body of Wesleyan Methodists, or of new sects established by ex-Methodists. Among the latter the most notable were the O'Bryanites in Cornwall, who in 1815 merged with the followers of James Thorne, a Devon farmer, to form the Bible Christian Connexion, and the Primitive Methodists, formed in 1811 by a merger of the followers of Hugh Bourne and William Clowes in north Staffordshire. But there were many shorter-lived groups, including the Tent Methodists, based in the Bristol area, who established a separate existence in 1820; the Band Room Methodists who had flourished a few years earlier in Manchester; the Magic Methodists of Cheshire; and at the opposite theological pole, the Cookeites or Unitarian Methodists of north-east Lancashire.

And both in Protestant and Catholic areas each parish had its distinctive traditions of fervour or apathy. In Saxony at the end of the nineteenth century and the beginning of the twentieth it was noted that there were still enormous local variations in church-going customs – in one parish regular church-going would be the norm, and in the next, half an hour's walk away, it was not, perhaps because of the personality of the pastor, perhaps because of a habit established many generations ago. In France the best recipe for a long-lasting anti-clerical tradition seems to have been the presence of a large land-owning monastery before the Revolution.[6]

Besides the innumerable local peculiarities of religious forms, there were also great differences between one country and another or one area and another in the extent and the nature of church influence. One reason for this was the very uneven penetration of the countryside achieved by the official churches. At the beginning of the nineteenth century, small market towns and prosperous agricultural areas tended to be well provided with churches and priests, but the remoter rural areas were often neglected as much as the new industrial zones. In England, Scotland and the Nordic countries evangelical missionaries were bringing Christianity to populations hitherto largely isolated from institutional religion. In France areas of forest or marsh often had few churches before the mid-nineteenth century. In Ireland the east was better provided with priests and churches than the poorer west. In these poorer areas lack of money for buildings and clergy meant that parishes, like those in north-western Scotland, were often 'so Extensive as to render the charge of them resemble a Province'.[7] The problem was often exacerbated by a lack of priests and preachers fluent in the local language. The costs of education required that the majority of clergymen come from a moderately prosperous background, and in the early nineteenth century they tended to be recruited in the more advanced areas of their countries. There was thus a relative shortage of Welsh-speaking clergy in the Welsh church, Gaelic-speakers in the Scottish church, Irish speakers in the Irish Church, Breton speakers in the French church.[8] These remote areas might, like the west of Ireland, be centres of a flourishing 'folk Catholicism', to whose pilgrimages, saints' day celebrations and wakes the priests were fairly peripheral. In parts of northern Scotland, however, where there were similar deficiencies in the ecclesiastical machinery, it seems that there was little knowledge at all of Christianity before the evangelistic and educational movements of the eighteenth and nineteenth centuries.

In contrast were areas like Bavaria where, at the beginning of the nineteenth century, the Counter-Reformation had done its work, and the secularising forces of the Enlightenment and the Revolution had as yet had little effect on the Catholic loyalty of the overwhelming majority of the rural population. A typical parish report of 1797 in the Munich diocese stated that scarcely 10 parishioners in a 1,000 missed Sunday mass. Others stressed the regularity with which their parishioners received the sacraments and attended special devotions. Catholicism was integrated into all areas of life. Catholic saints' days were the times of common relaxation; pilgrimages were necessary for the general well-being – God, it was believed, gave good harvests and good health to those who honour him. The church was a very big landowner until the French-imposed secularisation of 1803, but relations with tenants and with the numerous church employees seem to have been good; it was also responsible for the care of the sick and relief of the poor.

From about the 1820s, divergences appeared within the rural population, as some groups became conspicuously detached from the church. But when in the 1850s one of Le Play's collaborators studied a mountain parish in Upper Bavaria, he still found that the population of small farmers and lute-makers was devoutly Catholic. Every household had a shrine just inside the door, and the perhaps exceptionally devout family that provided the subject of the monograph went to mass daily, held prayers every evening, never worked on Sundays or feast days (believing that such work could bring no reward), made an annual pilgrimage, and contributed large sums to the church.[9] Of course, the realities of individual belief that lay behind the façade of religious unity were very hard for contemporary observers, let alone historians writing a century later, to gauge. Le Play noted the high rates of illegitimacy which showed the limits of the influence of official Catholic morality even in Mittenwald. In its combination of high levels, both of religious practice and of illegitimacy, it seems to have been typical of many Catholic areas of Germany in the first half of the nineteenth century. A more drastic break with church teaching seems to have taken place in such devout but impoverished regions of France as Brittany and the Massif Central, where infanticide was widely practised in the eighteenth and nineteenth centuries.[10] In some countries, such as Ireland, the clergy seem to have achieved a good deal of success by the nineteenth century in imposing general observance of Catholic sexual ethics (though attempts to control revolutionary violence were less successful). But everywhere, however attached to their churches the rural population appeared to be, the church was only one among several influences on their codes of behaviour, and church morality was continually modified by economic necessity, local tradition, the exigencies of social and political conflict. Similarly in matters of dogma: around 1700 a priest in the diocese of Tournai in northern France had complained that while none of his parishioners would be capable of refuting the doctrines taught from the pulpit, 'there are still some who hold in their hearts old errors that they could defend only on the grounds that they heard it from their fathers, and which they stubbornly maintain, as for instance that it is possible to be saved in any religion, etc.'.[11] A century and a half later Lutheran pastors in central Germany were complaining that apparently devout parishioners had no understanding of official teaching on such subjects as the fallen nature of man, or the eucharist. While in Hanover there were complaints that the people took the future life too much for granted, in some parts of Saxony it was said that the peasants had little belief at all in a life after death: 'They believe, pray, go to church, in order to obtain God's protection and help in this earthly life.' The author of these comments thought that peasant religion had a more pietistic flavour in the mountainous south of Saxony, where there was a strong mood of submission to the will of God in the face of misfortune.[12]

However, differences in social structure and in social relationships were an important differentiating factor, and would become very much more so in the course of the nineteenth century. Certainly in England it is unlikely that the kind of uniform orthodox piety described by Le Play could have been found anywhere but in the 'close' parish dominated by a large landowner. In these parishes the population was under pressure to follow the squire's lead in religion and politics, and this generally meant attending the Anglican church. Local studies in the East Midlands have found that Anglican attendance was highest in parishes with a resident squire.[13] The contrast between these tightly controlled communities and the freer and rougher 'open' village or isolated hamlet was graphically brought out in Flora Thompson's classic memoir of Oxfordshire hamlet life in the 1880s. Those like her radical and anti-clerical father had no wish to enjoy the benefits of paternalism, such as a rent free cottage, feeling that: 'A shilling or two shillings a week . . . was not too much to pay for the freedom to live and vote as they liked and to go to church or chapel or neither as they preferred.' But one Sunday morning, while their neighbours were sleeping, or cooking, or reading the newspaper, or admiring one another's pigs, they took a cart into a nearby town to visit a relative: 'Towards midday they passed through a village where the people, in their Sunday best were streaming towards the lych-gate of the church. The squire and the farmers wore top hats, and the squire's head gardener and the schoolmaster and the village carpenter. The farm labourers wore bowlers, or, the older men, soft round black felts.' It was a model village. 'Only good people were allowed to live there, her father said. That was why so many were going to church.'[14] But as far back as the 1690s the effective lapsing of the legal obligation to attend the parish church seems to have led to a drop in the number of church-goers and communicants in many areas, and so far as the evidence allows any confident conclusions, the consensus of eighteenth-century historians seems to be that the hold of the Anglican church on the English rural population was rather weak, even in the south and east which were relatively well provided with churches and clergy. Where specific sections of the population were picked out as conspicuous non-attenders it was generally the poor. For instance at the Oxford diocesan visitation in 1802 incumbents were asked: 'Are there any persons who absent themselves from all Public Worship? and from what motives or principles are they understood to do?' Many replied that there were no such people, but among those who said that there were, a typical comment was that of the vicar of Ducklington: 'The principal people are generally regular in their attendance in public worship. Of the lower order there are too many who pay too little attention to it. I should hope their poverty rather than any professed irreligious motive is the occasion.' Apart, then from the weaknesses of the Anglican parochial machinery, it would seem that the church's position was weakened by the high degree of social differentiation in rural society, and the rarity of the relatively egalitarian local social setting which provided a good basis for religious consensus in some parts of the continent.

II

While Protestant and Catholic countries were alike in the unevenness with which the official church had established itself, and in the difficulties they faced in areas of greatest social inequality, there were important respects in which Protestant countries were distinctive. One was the prevalence of sectarianism, another was in the different relationship between religion and magic. In Catholic countries these remained tightly bound together; throughout the nineteenth century and well into the twentieth many Catholics who were violently anti-clerical and never went to mass continued to turn to the saints in times of need, to ascribe supernatural potency to the church's sacraments, holy days, buildings – and indeed priests. In the 1950s and 1960s, the rural population of areas like Andalusia and southern Portugal, which had long been violently hostile to the church, still retained a belief in the curative powers of the saints, and many of them preferred the help of wise-women claiming God-given powers to that of the chemists and doctors. A century earlier the notoriously anti-clerical peasants of the Beauce were tightly wedded to a complex of rituals and taboos drawing upon Catholic symbols. Official Catholicism divided all areas of experience into sacred and profane – those that had special access to the holy, and those that made up part of the workaday world. Priests and nuns were closer than ordinary men and women; certain days of the year or periods, such as Holy Week, had a sacred character; the sacraments of the church were points of contact with the holy; certain buildings had been consecrated by the church; above all there were the saints, human, yet in immediate connection with God, so that every place or object associated with a saint provided a point of contact. From the clergy's point of view the holy offered above all aid in the purification of the soul and fight against sin; from the point of view of many ordinary Catholics, pious or impious, it offered access to supernatural help in all the problem areas of daily life. Priests were themselves widely credited with curative powers and control over the weather. In most of the Catholic countries of Europe relations between priest and people were indeed complex and many-sided. Seldom, in rural areas at least, were (or are) feelings towards the clergy purely neutral. Love, hatred, respect, fear, pride, contempt – these were the kinds of emotions rural Catholics felt, and sometimes they felt all of them at once. They gave vent to their obsession, and found some relief from their fears in a vast folklore of jokes about clerical lust and cynical comment about clerical greed. The more savage anti-clericals took on some of the aura that surrounded the enemy: so that the inhabitants of St. Chinian, a small town in the Hérault where five refractory priests were murdered in 1793, were locally nicknamed 'the eaters of priests' ears' and in the Spanish civil war legend had it that the Communist orator, Dolores Ibarruri, went one better and bit out the throats of captured priests.[15] Crop failures and storms were attributed by peasants to the malice of priests; conversely the priest's blessing was often considered essential to the well-being of an enterprise. Above all this meant that children were baptised and even the worst Catholic would often send for a priest if he thought he was dying. But priests were also called upon to bless crops, animals, mines: in 1840 a reforming priest in the Var found himself the target of charivari, when he refused to bless the oxen. During the same period in many parts of France priests found themselves in trouble with their parishioners because they refused to preside over the burial of men whom they believed to be infidels or conspicuous sinners. In one small town in the Var, in 1847, a crowd of 200 forced the door of the church so that a funeral ceremony, with prayers and holy water, could be held inside, in spite of the priest's refusal to participate. As Agulhon comments, the church held that Christian burial was for Christians, but:

The people claimed it for everyone: in the name of an unstated, but strongly held doctrine, according to which death needed *in itself* to be solemnised, they asserted that everyone had an equal right to the religious ceremonies of which the church was the normal provider, and that it abused its powers when it denied this right for doctrinal or moral reasons. As we have seen there was really a great indifference in religious matters, a profound implicit agnosticism behind this attachment to religious rites which had once been so striking. In terms of this popular outlook the underlying religion was the non-dogmatic cult of the dead, and the church was a machine for ceremonies, especially funeral ceremonies. By a curious paradox it was thus the church which then upheld the modern position according to which Catholicism is one option among others, and it was its opponents, the forerunners of the popular secular Left, who wanted the church to be a public service.[16]

Even where antagonism to the clergy was most bitter, the days and the objects consecrated by the church retained some of their potency. But above all processions, pilgrimages, and the cult of the saints generally provided the main focus of the religion of many rural Catholics, and drew in those whose ties with the church were otherwise rather loose. Certainly in the first half of the century, and in many areas for very much longer, processions and pilgrimages had a communal and social aspect going beyond their strictly religious meaning: they were expressions of common identity and occasions for general celebrations which were the property of the people as a whole, and not just of the devout. Furthermore since devotions of these kinds were often largely independent of the clergy, or even in defiance of the clergy, the many Catholics who were hostile to the church but not in any sense dogmatic atheists could participate without scruples. Those Catholics who saw the church mainly as a political institution and for whom God seemed distant and terrifying, could find comfort in Mary the universal mother, could identify themselves with a local or personal patron saint, or could turn without feeling that they were wasting his time to a saint who was known to specialise in particular types of problem or in the protection of particular animals or occupational groups. Catholics had a strongly personal relationship with their saints, and they developed a strong feel for the temperament, the eccentricities and the special talents of each. Favours accorded by the saint provided the basis for a life-long devotion; on the other hand, saints who failed to deliver found that business was certainly transferred elsewhere, and revenge might well be wreaked on their images. As has been pointed out by students both of Renaissance Italy and of present-day Naples, the cult of the saints is especially congruent with the framework of assumptions of a society based on patronage. It may also be seen as a particular manifestation in the terms of a given culture of a more general need of the individual to give meaning to areas beyond his control and understanding, by the personification of the forces controlling his life, and to extend his own existence by identifying with men and women both like himself and greater than himself.

In Protestant countries, however, the cult of the Virgin and the Saints had been replaced by the single cult of Jesus, the mass of sacred days had given way to the one 'Lord's Day'. Under the new regime religious observances may still have been the means of winning divine protection: Rudolf Braun sums up the peasant piety of the Zurich Oberland in the form of a bargain, 'I'll go to church for you if you'll keep the hail-stones away for me'; and in 1882 when hail-storms severely damaged the crops in one part of Württemberg, it seems that the peasants did reply by boycotting the church.[17] But the one major study of the relationship between religion and magic in a nineteenth-century rural Protestant environment, Obelkevich's book on Lincolnshire, suggests that the two had become substantially separated. Clergymen were still sometimes credited with supernatural powers, but they certainly did nothing to encourage such beliefs, and it seems to have been only rarely that they were called upon. Some of the rites of the church, notably churching, still had a superstitious significance, as did some of the days in the church's calendar. But for the most part the rituals and the remedies by which the rural population hoped to ward off the dangers surrounding them had no connection with the church. The clergy also had rivals in the handling of the supernatural in the form of the wise men, with talents for fortune-telling, divination and lifting spells: the small town of Louth, for instance, a great centre of Methodism, was equally famous for its wise men, whom villagers would come from miles around to consult. Obelkevich concludes that: 'popular Protestantism worked paradoxically to bring about the demystification of Christianity – particularly of the sacraments – while leaving nature still saturated with magical forces.'[18]

This analysis gains some support from studies of Lutheran Saxony in the nineteenth century and of the Calvinist Cévennes in the nineteenth and twentieth. Both stressed the central role of magic in the lives of the rural population; but both implied that it had become largely detached from the Protestant church. Thus Drews, writing of Saxony in 1902, claimed that: 'Superstition can only be rightly evaluated if it is seen as the real religion of the people. Generally speaking it is the unofficial religion standing over against the official church-Christian religion.'[19] And in a striking illustration of the Protestant church's lack of magical potency a Cévennes pastor complained in 1845 that in times of trouble some of his parishioners would travel to a neighbouring Catholic village to get the priest to say a mass for them.[20] Nonetheless the village conjurors who take the place of a clergy believing only in prayer and science are themselves often devout Protestants, and claim that their powers are God-given. There have always been many Protestant sects whose preachers believed as much in the everyday reality of miracles as any

Ultramontane priest. If the rationalisation of religion by the Protestant clergy took away some of the church's popular appeal, it would seem from the accounts by Joutard and Drews that many Protestant peasants happily combined the official 'religion' and the unofficial 'superstition', and saw no conflict between the two.

III

A further difference between Protestant and Catholic Europe lay in the strength of sectarianism in Protestant countries – a strength that greatly increased during the nineteenth century. Thus the important community-centre functions occupied by the parish church even in the most anti-clerical of Catholic regions were fulfilled by a variety of denominations, each with its own distinctive cultural emphases.

First of all it was a matter of pride for many rural communities to have their own church and priest. It did not follow from this that they intended to spend a lot of time there or make a lot of use of his services. But their existence enhanced the people's feeling of their own worth. In 1851, at a time when many parishes in France were getting their own priest for the first time since the Revolution, the *curé* of Châlons-sur-Marne complained that in parishes that had built a presbytery at great cost the *curé* arrived to find that no-one turned up for mass. In one such case the villagers of Futeau in the Argonne, very few of whom went to mass in the neighbouring village which did have a church, had been demanding their own church even in the year 1793; when, in 1848, they finally got one, only a small minority of the population did their Easter Duties, but the statues of the Virgin, St. Joseph, St. Eloi and St. Nicholas which the energetic *curé* erected were 'more revered than God himself'.[21] This same identification between the community and its church was perhaps reflected in the custom of ringing the church bells to abate storms – a custom reintroduced by popular demand by the anti-clerical municipality in one Haute-Vienne parish in 1885, after the priest had complied with a ban imposed by the prefect. During the Revolution bloody battles were sometimes fought when peasants tried to defend their churches from troops on the lookout for 'remnants of superstition' that could be melted down and converted to military use. In particular the community's identity was bound up with its local Virgin or saint, and the annual procession in which the saint was carried through the streets, or up a nearby mountain, was a solemn and festive occasion, bringing the whole population together. There was nothing illogical in the behaviour of the men in an Hérault parish where the *curé* stated in 1907: 'Not a single man does his Easter Duties, but it's a curious fact that they all take part in the processions.'[22] The other special focus of sacred feeling and communal identity was the parish cemetery, where former generations were buried.

A rather paradoxical expression of this same sense of identification with the parish church was the bitter opposition sometimes met by Anglican clergymen in the nineteenth century when they attempted to introduce more 'ritualistic' decorations and forms of services. One particularly potent pair of symbols was the church orchestra (an independent minded group, often of local craftsmen, with its own *esprit de corps* and tendencies to insubordination, and musical techniques which pained the fastidious) as against the organ or harmonium (often played by the schoolteacher or the squire's daughter, who provided more orderly and 'reverent' styles of music under firm clerical direction). The suppressions of the church orchestras in the middle years of the nineteenth century were often bitterly contested. Sometimes the musicians merely boycotted the church or went over en bloc to the Methodists. Elsewhere they stayed on to interrupt the choir or harmonium player who had taken their place, pelted their successors in the streets, or attacked the vicarage. At Little Walsingham in Norfolk they took more decisive action: on Guy Fawkes Day, 1865, they placed a large amount of gunpowder under the new organ, and blew it up. Whatever the clergy may have thought of the church orchestras it seems that their performances were often a big drawing point as far as the parishioners – and sometimes those of neighbouring parishes – were concerned. Like the Nonconformist chapels they gave ordinary villagers the chance to take star roles in the service, and one in which they had a certain amount of autonomy, and so strengthened their sense of belonging. 'Popish' innovations, such as vestments, candles on the altar, incense, also provoked violent opposition in many parts of England, the most famous example being the riots at St. George's in the East in the London dockland in 1856. At the Somerset village of Northmoor Common in 1866 a small group of men and women wearing paper 'vestments' entered the church during the service and started doing exaggerated imitations of the rituals performed by the high church vicar. The 'rioters' may often have been enjoying the opportunity of a bit of licensed hooliganism, rather than making a religious protest; but the fact that their actions were licensed by more staid members of the population reflected the fact that they felt that the church belonged to them, and what went on in it was their own business.[23]

In some parts of Britain the chapel became the *de facto* parish church. Though the moral exclusiveness of the Protestant sect was perhaps a greater barrier to general participation than the political and social exclusiveness of the official church, in some of the remoter areas one form or another of religious dissent managed to place its stamp on the culture of the whole population below the level of the gentry. In the north-west of Scotland it was the Free Church which, from its inception in 1843, was the central institution of the crofting population and was 'largely instrumental in welding a disparate collection of small tenants into a community capable of acting collectively and possessing a distinctive character and outlook'. In the Welsh-speaking areas of Wales, both industrial and agricultural, it was the Baptist, Independent and Calvinistic Methodist chapels. In many parts of Cornwall Methodism had achieved a similar position of dominance by about the 1840s. As Methodism grew from being a small sect to being one of the most powerful forces in Cornish life it necessarily came into conflict with an older pattern of recreation in which such activities as wrestling and cock-fighting were prominent, and drink was always an integral part. Sometimes Methodists came along to preach. More often they simply offered counter-attractions deliberately scheduled to co-incide with fairs and parish feasts – monster tea-drinkings, hymn-singings, processions. By 1844 it was claimed that the Camborne Whit Fair was a shadow of its former self, as far more people had chosen to go to the Redruth Tee-total and Rechabite festival. Not that the attempt to remould local culture was ever completely successful: apart from those who remained entirely unmoved by Methodism, and those who were very much on the margins of chapel life, there were many Methodists whose mores reflected an uneasy compromise between new and old. Jokes about the drinking habits of local preachers were as numerous as those about the sex lives of Catholic priests: no doubt many of the stories were more a form of revenge on these arbiters of morality than the literal truth – but they reflect the important point that moral revolutions however triumphant on the surface, are often much more fragile at ground level. The traditional Cornish crimes of smuggling and wrecking (plundering wrecked vessels), though both condemned by Wesley, also continued to be widely practised by Methodists, as well as by other Cornishmen.[24]

As will have become apparent this sense of identity between rural dwellers and their parish church did not necessarily include the priest or minister. Individual clergymen naturally evoked a wide range of personal responses and many of them were up to their necks in personal feuds; in some areas there was a general antagonism between the clergy and particular sections of the local population. But when the clergy were under attack they could find many parishioners not otherwise known for their piety coming to their defence, and for some embattled minorities the priest became a symbol of the identity of the whole group. In countries occupied by the French during the revolutionary wars, priests were among the leaders of national resistance – most notably in Spain, where there were few alternative leaders. Perhaps the outstanding example of priests as community leaders was Ireland.

IV

Much of what has been said here about the religious situation in rural Europe in the early nineteenth century remained true for a good while longer. Change was slow. But gradually the processes of centralisation and of technological progress had their effect, undermining local cultures, bringing in new ideas, rendering old customs obsolete. Equally important were changing patterns of economic relationships, disrupting existing patterns of community. It has become an historical cliché that these changes often spelt 'dechristianisation'. Even more important in the shorter run were the processes of 'christianisation' or 'rechristianisation' which were on the march in many parts of western Europe during the early and middle decades of the nineteenth century. In the longer run, as far as most of Europe was concerned, it was probably not so much the revival or the destruction of Christianity that was most significant, but the change in the character of religion and the social context within which it operated.

The processes of christianisation and rechristianisation were fuelled partly by movements of religious revival, which spurred men and women to devote their lives to evangelistic and charitable work; partly by sectarian revalry; partly by the fears of threatened élites, hoping that religion might act as a social sedative; partly by material progress, offering the resources to support the building of thousands of churches and schools, the payment of tens of thousands of priests, nuns and other religious workers.

For much of the nineteenth century churches were being built in remote areas; long neglected parishes were being revitalised; new religious orders were being formed in Catholic countries, and intensive missionary work was being concentrated on areas alienated from the church; in Protestant countries the first half of the nineteenth century was the great age of revival movements, and these too were often especially active in areas where the church had had little influence. The first six or seven decades of the nineteenth century were the years when the French church tried to make good the losses inflicted by the Revolution, and the Irish church those inflicted by the penal laws; the English church reformed itself after long years of decay, and in England, Scotland, and Scandinavia, revival movements both inside and outside the state churches, took Christianity to the remotest northern wastes.

Reconstruction was most successful in Ireland, where by the end of the century there had, from the point of view of the Roman Catholic authorities, been substantial improvements in every quantifiable area of Catholic life: attendance at mass was much higher; the number of priests and nuns had increased (in spite of a declining population); there were more churches, bigger churches, more richly decorated, and in better repair. It was in rural areas, especially the remoter western counties, that the improvement had been most striking, for it had been in those areas that the church had been weakest earlier in the century. There had also been an important qualitative change, in that the Catholicism of the later nineteenth century was more orthodox and more clerically controlled.

In France the effects of reconstruction were much patchier. The church consolidated its hold on areas like the Massif Central, where it was already strong. On the other hand, in some of the *départements* round Paris the church machinery never recovered from the Revolution. The network of pastoral care, charitable institutions, catechists, confraternities, church buildings was never effectively repaired after the destruction of the 1790s. Meanwhile, in some remote forest, marsh, or coastal fishing communities, Catholic parishes were being formed for the first time in the middle years of the nineteenth century. In areas like Guînes, near Calais, where in 1877 'the wild men of the marsh' were still said to live 'isolated, without religion, speaking who knows what language', Hilaire comments that Catholicism and 'civilisation' tended to advance together.[25] In 1912 George Bourne made a similar point in his study of a heathland community in Surrey, where the church, far from being a relic of a former age, was seen as one of the forces for change in an area where organised religion had never played much part:

it should be remembered that until some time after the enclosure of the common the village had no place of worship of any denomination. Moreover the comparatively few inhabitants of that time were free from interference by rich people or by resident employers. They had the valley to themselves; they had always lived as they liked, and been as rough as they liked . . . We may therefore surmise that when the church was built a sprinkling at least of the villagers were none too well pleased. This may partly explain the sullen hostility of which the clergy are still the objects in certain quarters of the village, and which the Pharisaism of some of their friends does much to keep alive. The same causes may have something to do with the fact that the majority of the labouring men take no interest at all in religion. Still, there are more than a few young men, and of old village stock too, who yield very readily to the influences of the Church.[26]

This influence he detected mainly in a 'softening of manners', strong ethical views, and adoption of middle-class values, though he saw equally important forces for change in the newspapers, mostly of the ' "yellow-press" kind', as a result of which 'a standardised sentiment is growing among the villages', and in the growing interest of some villagers in politics, the correlates of which were a more 'scientific' outlook and an interest in their children's education.

In many parts of western Europe this effort of institutional reconstruction was running out of steam in the last quarter of the nineteenth century. In France the turning-point was the accession to power in 1877–9 of the anti-clerical republicans. In Britain at the same time religious indifference was spreading in the upper and middle classes; sectarian rivalry was declining. By the 1890s the rise in the number of Anglican clergymen and church buildings (continuous and substantial since the 1830s) was flattening out; the number of ordinations reached a peak in 1886 and thereafter fell sharply. From the 1880s membership of the English Nonconformist churches was failing to keep pace with the rise in population; meanwhile the increasing pace of defections to Anglicanism among their wealthier members was causing financial problems for many chapels.

But long before the end of the nineteenth century there were forces of 'dechristianisation' at work in the countryside. Mass alienation from the national church was already apparent in England in the early nineteenth century, in north-eastern France around the middle of the century, and in the northern Netherlands in the 1880s. In each of these areas the bigger farms were growing, the smallholders were becoming labourers, social distance was increasing, and the landless or near-landless majority of the population gave up worshipping beside the employers whom they hated and who held them in contempt. The change was most drastic in areas dominated by large estates, where there was an unbridgeable gulf between a small, very wealthy landowning élite and the mass of poor labourers.

Studies by anthropologists of rural communities in various parts of the Iberian peninsula in the 1950s and 1960s brought out the contrast very clearly. On the one hand we have Cutileiro's study of a group of villages dominated by large landowners in south-east Portugal and Pitt-Rivers' book on Grazalema, a former Anarchist stronghold among the latifundia of Andalusia; on the other, Christian's account of the Nansa valley high up in the Cantabrician mountains of northern Spain. Part of the church's weakness in the former areas may lie simply in neglect or in the adverse effects of anti-clerical government policies: in both Spain and Portugal the ratio of priests and people has for long been much worse in the south than in the north, and as a result many parishes have gone through long periods without a resident priest, or with too few priests to minister effectively to a scattered population. But there is clearly more to it than that. In both areas attitudes to the church are strongly affected by class, and among the impoverished majority there is often a positive hatred of the church. In the Portuguese parish, where 'the legitimacy of the division of land' was 'often totally denied' and the Communist Party had a lot of support, the priest was on close terms with the small group of large landowners, who were among the few men who ever did their Easter duties. In 1965, indeed, only 2 men and 11 women out of a population of 1,600 had confessed during the year. This area had not seen any of the violence against the priests that had been characteristic of southern Portugal between 1911 and 1926, but even the women, who, unlike the men, would insist that they were Catholics, said that the priests were not. In Grazalema, the small élite was highly integrated and shared 'certain common standards of conduct, the most important of which is their adherence to the church'. As far as the rest of the population were concerned, belief in the Virgin and the saints was strong, belief in the church and the clergy weak, especially among the men. Pitt-Rivers comments that the devout of whatever class are women: men see the church mainly as a social and political institution, the *señoritos* going to church because they associate it with the Right, and the men of the people staying away for the same reason. In the village in the Nansa valley, some people (most of them women) were more devout than others, but there were no alienated classes, and everyone was to some degree integrated into the life of the parish. A precondition for this situation was a completely different social structure. While the shopkeepers and professionals formed something of a group apart, most of the people were occupied in raising cattle, partly on privately owned pastures, and partly in communal meadows high up on the mountains. Some families had bigger herds than others, but these differences were not wide enough to lead to the formation of opposing social classes. Village questions were decided by village meetings, with all families represented. Village priests, according to Christian, see themselves as mediators, dedicated to the cause of social unity: here the ground is well laid for them, whereas in Andalusia real unity would be impossible because of the completely unequal distribution of power. In such a situation the mediator inevitably ends up on one side or the other; and the result of the choice that they made was a long history of church-burnings and priest-killings. In the Nansa valley the corresponding tradition is of the opposite kind: the memory of the early months of the civil war when the northern coastal belt was in Republican territory, and the loyal Catholics had to protect their priests and their saints.[27]

While the areas of most blatant social inequality seem invariably to have experienced a mass alienation from the official church in the nineteenth century, the situation was much more varied in those places where land ownership was more evenly distributed. In France these included both Catholic strongholds, like the southern Massif Central, and areas of dechristianisation, like the externally very similar hamlets of the nearby Limousin. In many cases, as in the Limousin, the decline of the church went hand in hand with political radicalism. The reasons for these highly varied patterns have to be determined by detailed local investigation. Only one factor is clearly established: the fact that a number of these dechristianised areas were, like the La Rochelle region, former Protestant strongholds, converted to Catholicism under Louis XIV by such techniques as the quartering of troops on 'heretical' families – methods that achieved the short-term aim of killing Protestantism, but failed in the longer-term objective of making good Catholics.

V

Technological changes may have changed the nature of rural religion and sometimes reduced its scope, but they did not of themselves lead to any mass detachment from the church of the sort found in southern Spain. We should not take too literally the Dutch saying that 'artificial fertilisers make atheists'.[28] We have in fact several different processes of religious decline in parts of rural Europe during the nineteenth and early twentieth centuries: a decline of magic, a decline of the church and a decline of Christianity. And the three do not necessarily go together. The decline of the church was first in evidence, the main reason being the resentment of the rural poor against a church which they saw as an ally of the dominant classes. They did not thereby become any more rational in their view of the world, and they did not necessarily become any less Christian: in their view it might well be the farmers and the clergy who were the bad Christians. Only when a variety of doctrines of secular salvation – from Jacobinism, to socialism, anarchism and Fascism – come forward to give form to this can we speak of a general decline of Christianity, and even then there was a longstanding tendency for the rank and file of many of these movements to interpret them as 'true Christianity'.[29] The decline of magic was a later, more long drawn out, and more general process, which changed the devout areas as much as the irreligious, but did not necessarily make them any less devout. Indeed the decline of magic may even have been slower in less devout areas, where the people were less subjected to newer ideas of religion. In 1960 priests of the Mission de France, whose job was to evangelise areas of minimal religious practice, found that in the south-west they were being asked to bless corn and say masses for sick pigs, and candles were being taken from the church because they were thought to provide protection from storms.[30]

The characteristic development of the later nineteenth and early twentieth centuries was the incursion on many isolated rural communities of a pluralist society in which consensus had broken down, and a variety of ways of living were possible. There is a brilliant account of the ways in which this could happen in Roger Thabault's *Mon Village*, the story of Mazières-en-Gâtine, a backward commune in the Deux-Sèvres *département* of western France, which entered around 1860 on a period of rapid social change. The basic factors identified by Thabault were improved communications with the outside world and the increasing involvement of the agricultural population in production for the market. The results of these developments were more contact with new ideas, and new aspirations that led the people to question many deep-rooted assumptions, and sometimes to reject the church, which seemed to stand as a barrier to the realisation of their hopes. One symptom and cause of change was the politicisation of the commune in the late 1870s by a bourgeois landowner of violently anti-clerical views, who for the first time challenged the authority of the *seigneur*. More generally Thabault suggested that a new 'religion of progress' was transforming the outlook of many people at this time, its chief exponents being the teachers in the secular school, and its main tenets being patriotism, republican politics, and a desire for one's children to get ahead. Studies of Protestant Germany around the end of the nineteenth century also tend to mention the breakdown of rural isolation and the fact that this was usually followed by a weakening of church influence. Here the influence of the highly secularised towns was felt not only through the propaganda of the Social Democrats and the formation in the villages of the innumerable *Vereine* (associations for sport, music, shooting, etc.), which had once been an exclusively urban phenomenon, but also through the growing tendency for smallholders to spend Monday to Saturday working in a nearby town – one consequence of which was a labour shortage on the farms which encouraged the middle-peasant to spend Sunday in the fields rather than in church.

The most colourful analysis of these processes appears in Eugen Weber's study of the transformation of rural France between 1871 and 1914. Chemical fertilisers obviated the need for church rituals; quinine had put St. Viatre (a specialist in curing malaria) out of a job; the cult of local saints was under attack both from church authorities and from anti-clerical municipal officials; new secular holidays, like 14 July, were supplementing the old saints' days; peasants who did not want to have to split up the family inheritance between a numerous progeny were practising *coitus interruptus*, in spite of clerical condemnation; pictures of the saints were making place on farmhouse walls for giant illustrations, from the *Petit Journal's* illustrated supplement, of shipwrecks and mining disasters; dancing for the young, cafés for the men, newspapers for everyone, were providing new forms of entertainment, which again could lead to conflict with the clergy. Weber places all of these events within a fairly simple progressive secularisation framework. His chapter entitled 'Dieu est-il Français?' ends as follows:

'*Monsieur le curé,*' said Norre, 'I've tried everything. I've had masses said and got no profit from them. I've bought chemicals and they worked. I'll stick to the better merchandise.' It was the requiem of nineteenth-century religion.[31]

A framework of change and adaptation would be preferable. The first point is that rural religion was in a process of continuous development. The obsolescence of older forms was often matched by the growth of new forms, which sometimes had a narrower appeal, but cannot simply be equated with 'decline'. So, as communal forms of religion were weakening, the proliferating organisations of the church-based sub-culture gave new support to the faith of the individual believer; and as improved technology made magic less necessary, increasing contact with the outside world made questions of personal salvation more urgent and problematic. Christian suggested that successive stages in the religious history of northern Spain were reflected in the existence side by side in the mountain villages of three quite different forms of Catholicism: a religion going back to medieval, and probably to pre-Christian times, that was focussed on the shrines of the saints, and on the search for protection from the vicissitudes of everyday life; a Tridentine Catholicism, directed primarily towards individual, other-worldly salvation; and a Vatican II Christianity, taught by the younger priests, which was most strongly concerned with inter-personal relations and social justice. In these villages it was only around 1900 that the second form of religion became widely established, and began to supersede the first.[32]

A second point is that in many parts of rural Europe the Catholic church adapted so successfully to social change in the later nineteenth and early twentieth century that it was able to maintain its institutional strength by making a selective takeover of the modernising forces. In Brittany in the early twentieth century we find priests managing the most popular daily paper, and the peasants buying their fertilisers from co-operatives whose local agent was very often the priest. In Lower Austria priests took a prominent part in the Christian Social Party, which had a large network of co-operatives and credit banks, and enjoyed overwhelming peasant support in elections. In Old Castile the organis-ation of the tenant farmers came mainly from the priests, and in the

1930s, Catholic loyalty would be the main factor turning the rural population of much of northern Spain against the Second Republic. When survivors of the civil war were interviewed in the 1970s, those on both sides in Old Castile saw the Republic's anti-clericalism as a fatal blunder. As the Falangist organiser of a sugar-beet growers' union put it, the peasants were not anti-republican a priori 'but because of what the republic turned out to be . . . Castile above all, was religious, patriarchal. It was not for nothing that the Castilian peasantry provided the bulk of Spain's priests, friars, nuns.'[33] So, as the countryside became integrated into a wider national community it was often the church which controlled its points of contact and provided the major defenders of its interests and symbols of its identity. In some French dioceses statistics of religious practice are available which show little change between the 1890s and 1950s.[34] In these rural strongholds it was only in the 1960s that the intrusion of styles of life current in the wider culture seriously threatened the influence of the church.

5 Urbanisation

I

In 1800 the population of every country in western Europe was heavily rural. The Netherlands (with 30 per cent of the population living in towns of over 10,000 people) represented the high point of urbanisation, while England and Wales (21 per cent), Scotland (17 per cent) and Belgium (14 per cent) were nearest. London, with 1 million people, was by far the largest city in Europe, while Paris was in second place with about 550,000. In Britain the proportion of a fast-growing population that lived in towns nearly doubled in the next fifty years, with London reaching about 2½ million people, and Manchester, Liverpool, Birmingham and Glasgow around the ¼ million mark. Elsewhere the big increase in urban growth came in the second half of the century. By 1890 Great Britain had a predominantly urban population, and the proportion in towns of over 10,000 exceeded 30 per cent in Belgium, Saxony and Prussia, as well as the Netherlands. Beside London (over 4 million) and Paris (2½ million), Berlin and Vienna now had over a million people, and cities of the second rank, like Hamburg, Manchester and Brussels, stood at ½–¾ million. In 1960 Paris and London stood at over 7 million, while about a dozen cities in western Europe had populations of over a million, and many others effectively formed conurbations of similar size. In Great Britain, the world's most urban country, the cities had long reached saturation point, and the most significant tendency was the increasing irrelevance of the rural/urban distinction, as most rural areas had become outposts of a single urban-dominated culture, and a single urban-based economy. In many other countries the depopulation of the countryside was still in progress in the years following the Second World War, and up into the 1960s it was still possible to speak of distinctively rural cultures.

The implications of these upheavals for religion were varied and contradictory. The character of religion changed as ever-larger proportions of the population lived in towns, and were employed in industry and commerce; at some points the very existence of the churches seemed to be threatened in the process. On the other hand the circumstances of life in the fast-growing urban zones of nineteenth-century Europe presented problems to which religion often appeared to offer the best solutions. The following section will look at three examples: the need for identity and mutual support; the need for moral order amid the surrounding chaos; the need for protection against a dangerous environment.

II

With the great movement of country people into the cities and industrial zones there went a great mixing of populations. Irishmen flooded into Liverpool, Glasgow and Sydney, Italians into Marseille and Buenos Aires, Flemish-speaking Belgians into Lille, Poles into the Ruhr, and Englishmen into the Rhondda. Catholic peasants left the villages of the Rhineland or North Brabant for Protestant-dominated cities, and the speakers of Breton, Provençal, Alsacien, and a hundred local patois, headed for Paris. Louis Wirth, in his famous essay on 'Urbanism as a way of life' presented the city as melting-pot, breeder of a sophisticated relativism. In the short-term, however, the tendency was usually in the opposite direction. Natives saw the newcomers not as a standing criticism of their own tribal mores, but as paddies and sheenies, *grenouilles* and *Schwarzen*.[1] And they in turn sought safety within their own ghettos. If the second generation was less at home in the ghetto, it often remained heavily stamped by its inheritance. In this situation priests and ministers were important spokesmen for ethnic communities, and churches were often the major bases for the immigrant's communal life and his sense of identity.

The nearest thing in nineteenth-century Europe to Chicago or Pitts–burgh was the Ruhrgebiet, the great zone of mining and heavy industry in western Germany. Up to about 1870 the labour force was drawn mainly from surrounding rural areas. But in the boom of 1870–3 the mining companies began to look eastwards. First the special trains brought in Germans from East and West Prussia. But from the early 1880s they were bringing Slavs – Masurians, Slovenes, and, above all, Poles. By 1907 it was said that twenty different languages and dialects were spoken in the Ruhr. And, just as in the many immigrant ghettos of the United States, the founding of churches like those they had left behind them was a primary concern of many of these uprooted workers. Many prayer groups or sectarian organisations were formed by Protestant immigrants from East Prussia; Roman Catholic immigrants, most notably the Poles, would begin by forming a St. Barbara Association, in honour of the patroness of miners. Then they would form a committee to press the diocesan authorities for a new parish, and when permission was obtained they would organise the collection of money to build a church.

The churches, for their part, often took the first initiatives in establishing workers' organisations for mutual support and sociability. In 1889–90 there were some 87 Roman Catholic and 61 Protestant workers' associations in the mining area. The greatest interest seems to have been in organisations offering death benefits; but there were also youth groups, clubs for workers from particular provinces, and rallies where Catholics could celebrate their religious identity. Catholic workers voted in large numbers for the Centre Party, and joined the Christian trade union, which around the turn of the century was in frequent conflict with the socialist-led union. Well into the twentieth century, those organisations, such as the Social Democrats, who wanted to unite the workers on the common ground of class had to compete with other equally powerful organisations emphasising their many divergent identities. And religion often played an important part in these.

The strength of the churches in the Ruhr arose partly from the effects of the mixing of many heterogeneous, and initially incompatible ethnic groups, but also from the fact that so many of the immigrants came from a strongly religious background – Polish Catholics, Masurian and East Prussian Lutherans, Calvinist sectarians from the neighbouring hills. But regardless of the religious background or convictions of the newcomer to the city, he might often find that churches held strategic positions within the patronage networks through which votes were collected, jobs, charity, individual or collective favours distributed. At its crudest the situation could be that described by one of Thompson and Vigne's respondents, an old woman, who had been born in a poor south London family in the 1890s:

'Yes, yes, you may as well have it, that – that's all we went to church for – to keep in with them and that. They were – they'd got the authority and we hadn't. They knew where to put the fingers on what was needed.' 'So you used them?' 'Yes. You had to. Go betweens. Yes.' 'How about chapel?' 'Oh they were all the same, they were on committees and all the same, they were on committees and all just the same.'[2]

And this was not very different from the advice proffered to aspiring clerks in 1893: 'A steady young man commencing life in Liverpool, without capital or good friends, cannot do better for his own business future than by joining and becoming active, useful and respected in a large dissenting congregation.'[3] But beyond the hard calculation of interest, there was the sense of common identity, the numerous ties of friendship and marriage, the communal pressures, that made such calculation generally superfluous. In nineteenth-century Europe religion often determined how people voted, how they spent their leisure hours, even which tradesmen they patronised, and where they worked. To be a Catholic, a Protestant – or, for that matter, a socialist – was not only to believe certain doctrines, and behave in certain prescribed ways, it was to belong to a community with its own strong sense of common identity, and vigorous pursuit of common interests.

In the Ruhr Protestant children fought Catholic children, while their parents dubbed the Catholics 'the blacks', and in the mainly Protestant town of Witten a Catholic neighbourhood was called the 'nigger village'. But by comparison with Ireland, southern France, or even some parts of Britain, sectarian antagonism seems to have taken relatively peaceful forms. It was in the silk city of Nîmes and the linen city of Belfast that two opposing social hierarchies founded on religious identity were brought into direct confrontation, and the results were orgies of sectarian killing quite unparalleled in western Europe's modern history. In Nîmes the Catholics had the numbers and the Protestants had the money; in Belfast the Protestants had the advantage in both respects. In both cities Protestant largely worked with and for Protestant, Catholic with and for Catholic. In both, political allegiances were largely determined by religion, and patronage always had a sectarian character. In Belfast, even sanitary officials were 'not always selected for their technical competence, but rather because they held prominent position in church or chapel and had been able to render eminent service at election times'.[4] In both cases urbanisation meant that two groups with long histories of mutual violence behind them were living side by side, competing for the same jobs, fighting for the ascendancy. For concentrated sectarian violence Nîmes probably holds the records, with several hundred Catholics dying in the pitched battle in the city in 1790 which initiated the first period of Protestant ascendancy, and about a hundred Protestants being killed by Catholic murder squads (and several thousands going into the mountains or fleeing the *département*, while others abjured their faith) in the summer of 1815. But for recurrent communal violence extending through the whole of this period nowhere in western Europe can match Belfast.

In both Ireland and south-eastern France, a long-persecuted religious community, with much to avenge, threatened as a result in one case of 1789, in the other of the movement to repeal the union with Great Britain, to claim political power, with all that this might mean for the formerly dominant group. In both instances the size of the Catholic threat made Protestants unusually willing to make common cause – though in Belfast there remained throughout the nineteenth century a significant minority of Protestants who remained true to the city's eighteenth-century liberalism, and refused to accept the new anti-Catholic consensus. In both cities there were rare occasions when social conflicts came to the fore and temporarily eclipsed sectarian consciousness. But nowhere did sectarian ties and considerations so overshadow all others. In the Ruhr, for instance, Catholic workers might prefer the Christian trade union to the socialist-led *Alter Verband*, but both unions were primarily concerned with improving the conditions of workers in general, and at times both would join in common action against employers; in Belfast, on the other hand, a major consideration of the skilled workers' unions was excluding Catholics. Elsewhere Protestants tended to think as conservatives, liberals, or socialists, rather than as Protestants, and while all of these might be to some degree anti-Catholic their differences with their co-religionists were at least as significant as their common antagonism towards the Catholic church.

Religion could also play an important part in the process by which some sort of moral order was established in the new working class communities. Nineteenth-century social commentators were often preoccupied with the breakdown of social discipline in the cities and industrial zones: the prevalence of crime, drunkenness, sexual promiscuity. Equally significant however was the development of new moral disciplines self-imposed by the proletarians themselves. Already in the 1820s some observers were talking of a moral revolution that had taken place within the working class in England during recent decades. In 1829 Francis Place claimed that in the last thirty years the working classes had 'become wiser, better, more frugal, more honest, more respectable, more virtuous than they ever were before', while James Mill had claimed three years earlier that 'gentleness' and 'civility' were replacing 'riot and drunkenness', and that there had been a 'prodigious amelioration' in 'manners' and 'moralities' within living memory. E.P.Thompson sums up the evidence by suggesting that between 1780 and 1830: 'The "average" English working man became more disciplined, more subject to the productive tempo of "the clock", more reserved and methodical, less violent and less spontaneous.'[5] The revolution was partly imposed from above – by a changed attitude on the part of the dominant classes, embodied in repressive legislation, stricter policing, factory discipline, and withdrawal of patronage from many popular amusements. But equally important was the revolution from below – the development within the working class of a public opinion which rejected as degraded and unworthy much of the existing popular culture, and saw the way forward as lying through industry, self-discipline, organisation, and above all education. Manifestations of this new trend included the boom in popular educational institutions, beginning with the rapid development of the Sunday School movement from the 1780s; the spread of friendly societies from the early nineteenth century; the development from the 1830s of the temperance movement; and throughout this period the rejection by a section of the working class of many traditional amusements involving violence, drunkenness, gambling or cruelty to animals. The change was epitomised in the democratisation of the concept of 'respectability', and the increasingly current distinction between a 'respectable' and a 'rough' working class. In the chaotic conditions of fast-growing industrial villages and working class suburbs churches and chapels were often strongholds of this 'respectable' working class. Robert Moore has shown how the prominence of drunkenness and violence in newly established Durham mining communities around the 1870s gave point to the temperance preaching of the Methodists: preaching which, by the 1920s and 1930s would seem exaggerated and irrelevant. A typical memory by one of the elderly Methodists whom Moore interviewed was that : 'Our father used to keep us in the house. One family used to come regularly to our house to sleep when the father was on the rampage. There was a lot of drinking.'[6] This same picture of the chapel as a haven of respectability in an environment where 'rough' or conspicuously anti-social forms of behaviour were oppressively familiar comes through in the autobiography of an east London cabinet-maker, published in 1911, and one of the most interesting working-class memoirs of the time. Street fights, rows, crime and heavy drinking are the staple fare of everyday life in Bethnal Green of the 1880s as he saw it as a child. And he explained his 'leaning towards religion' by the fact that: 'Places of worship were so clean that I often felt the desire to go into a local church. The brooding feeling of peacefulness seemed to smooth one's turbulent desires.' Later a friend persuaded him to go to Dorland Street chapel, 'probably the most important step I ever took in my life,' by saying: 'They don't preach at you much, no shouting about Jesus, or telling you what a wicked sinner you are, I believe they live good first, and influence you like by that.' And though he attributed a religious crisis that he subsequently went through to the rationalist books he had read, his religion is described very largely in terms of a new life-style, consisting of such activities as saving, reading books, and giving up drinking and gambling.[7] The Roman Catholic clergy in London also laid great stress on saving and on temperance, and though there were certainly many Catholics who took little notice of these injunctions – except perhaps during the period of religious excitement associated with the parish mission – there are some signs that the more committed members of the parish tended to adopt many of the values associated with their Protestant counterparts. For instance a Stepney priest interviewed by Charles Booth in the 1890s suggested that half the Catholics who came to mass were teetotallers, and a Fulham priest distinguished between the 'respectable poor' who 'attend well to their religious duties' and the 'rough poor' who 'do not'.[8] In Thompson and Vigne's interviews with those brought up in working-class families around the beginning of this century, similar themes frequently appear. Asked about the 'rough'/ 'respectable' distinction, one respondent, a Londoner born in 1904, whose parents were not themselves church-goers, said that the former were those who fought in the streets, while the latter were often church-goers; and the son of a Methodist joiner, living in the Potteries, said that some were considered rough because they drank, and others respectable because they went to church or chapel and were clean and tidy. A classic example of the latter kind of family was that described by a Bolton man, born in 1895. His father was an iron-moulder, a union man, and an active supporter of the temperance and co-operative movements. All the family attended the Anglican church. His mother was a strict disciplinarian, and she brought them up to be: 'God-fearing, respectable, law-abiding citizens. Respect for the law and respect for your parents. We were taught the ten commandments and they were pretty well drilled into us.' She would never ask for charity. He distinguished the 'respect-able working class' who had 'served their time at a particular trade' from 'the labouring class'. Among the latter: 'There were respectable labour-ers who would mix in various church activities, I suppose, who would be considered religious in the religious life of the church. You would mix with them, you wouldn't look down on them in any shape or form. The only people you would look down on was the people who used to get drunk and neglect their family life – their wives and children.'[9]

In Britain, at least, then, the desire for 'respectability' and a repudi-ation of 'rough' habits of life was often a major concern of working-class church-goers, and a strong attraction of church life seemed to be that it offered an orderly, self-respecting and independent style of life. Yet this desire could be two-edged so far as its religious implications were concerned, as it could lead working-class people to reject those churches which handed out charity, or where the minister encouraged attitudes of deference and subordination. Indeed a socialist secularist, like Robert Tressell, would claim that 'the "religious" working man type' consisted of 'tame, broken-spirited wretches' who 'went every Sunday afternoon to be lectured on their duties to their betters.'[10]

In the cities and industrial zones of nineteenth-century Europe, as much as on the farms, danger often brought religious revival, and supernatural help was sought in times of individual or collective crisis. The most striking example of this was the response to the terrible cholera epidemics which struck the continent between the 1830s and 1860s. Priests tended to explain the cholera as a scourge sent by God to punish the sins of the nation, or of particular sections of the population. The arrival of cholera in the neighbourhood certainly had the effect of concentrating the mind wonderfully. One result of this was the 'cholera revival' which occurred in some parts of Britain while the epidemics were in progress. In the Black Country, the belt of small towns and industrial villages lying between Birmingham and Wolverhampton, it was reported after the 1849 epidemic that:

Occasionally . . . as many as one or two hundred colliers would assemble, and in one instance as many as seven hundred; and after singing a hymn would remain on their knees for nearly an hour at a time, following the prayers of one of their local preachers (usually one of their own body), and lamenting aloud their own sinful lives, specifying their own particular failings, such as spending so much of their money in drink, and giving so little of it to their wives and families, and resolving to amend.

This mass repentance was reflected in the sharp increases in Methodist membership in both 1832 and 1849 in many parts of the Black Country. However, the promised amendment of life was often short-lived. The report on the miners at the time of the 1849 epidemic does indeed state that 'within a fortnight of the disappearance of the cholera these meetings began visibly to decline; . . . about six weeks after . . . many of them had been abandoned'. Recent research has discovered that by 1851 many circuits were back to pre-cholera memberships levels, though there were some that had made net gains over the period.[11] Meanwhile in Lille, the textile metropolis of northern France, the epidemic of 1832 led to pilgrimages, and public prayers round the statues of the Virgin that stood at many street corners.

III

While acute danger gave religious questions a sudden urgency for many individuals whose faith was at most times a fairly peripheral part of their lives, there were some cities where the whole population re-enacted the centuries-old rituals of collective devotion and repentance. In Marseille, where the cholera first arrived in the winter of 1834–5, the traditional Catholic processions, suppressed by the anti-clerical municipal authorities in 1832, were brought back by popular demand. A gigantic open-air mass in the centre of the city, the culmination of a long procession through the streets, was said to have been attended by everyone who had not already fled, or was not in bed. 'Imagine the whole length of the Cours', wrote a local paper, 'filled with an immense crowd, more than 30,000 Marseillais prostrated before the holy mysteries and even the windows of all the adjoining houses filled with spectators on their knees.'

The report went on to describe the cries of horror that came from every corner of the main street, from the windows and from the side-alleys, when, with a terrible crack, the platform on which the bishop was to celebrate mass collapsed, bringing down altar, bishop and many priests with it. However, no-one was badly hurt, and soon afterwards the epidemic came to an end.[12]

But the epidemics of the 1830s also showed that there were some cities where the symbols that had once served to unite the population in the face of disaster were now a source of division. In London a national day of fasting had been prescribed by Parliament in 1832: but while large numbers did attend the special service at St. Paul's (where many of them had to stand, because they could not pay for a seat), there were also well-attended radical demonstrations, where scorn was poured on the official observances, and the bishops were singled out for special attack. And in Paris, far from accepting either a medical or theological explanation for the epidemic, the people accused the government and the bourgeoisie of having poisoned the fountains, and some suggested that the clergy were part of the plot. Louis Chevalier refers to 'many demonstrations of irreligion' in the city during the outbreak, and when the Archbishop made a visit to the victims lying in hospital in the centre of the city, a contemporary wrote that:

In other times he would have had to push his way into the forecourt of the Hotel-Dieu through crowds prostrating themselves as he passed, imploring his blessing; but not so now. Their demeanour simply expressed indifference, defiance or fury. Neither priest nor sister was spared the most mendacious and atrocious accusations.

In Madrid in 1834 the reaction was the same: Jesuits and monks were rumoured to have poisoned the springs, and as a result religious buildings were burned down and some monks killed.[13]

Since the 1790s there had in fact been signs of a religious crisis in many of the cities of Europe. Though the churches continued to play a big part in urban life throughout the nineteenth century, and well into the twentieth, it was clear that the cities were centres of disaffection from the state churches, and sometimes of a generalised scepticism, and that the kind of religious unity demonstrated in Marseille in 1835 was increasingly the preserve of remote country areas. There were several distinct elements in this process: bourgeois anti-clericalism and the diffusion of 'the ideas of 1789'; the growth of vast new industrial suburbs largely without churches and priests; the increasing alienation of the working class from the other sections of the urban population, and the development of an independent working class sub-culture.

If we look in greater detail at the nineteenth-century evidence for urban irreligion, it becomes clear that the crisis took several distinct forms. Probably the sharpest contrast between town and countryside was to be found in some parts of Protestant Germany. By the end of the century very few Protestants went to church in the towns, whereas there were quite a lot of rural areas where as a Württemberg pastor stated in 1912: 'It is the established custom that, at least on Sunday morning, someone comes to church from each house.'[14] In Protestant Germany lack of involvement in the life of their church was a general facet of the urban population, though there were a few social groups, such as state officials and the lower middle class, who were sometimes singled out as being the mainstay of their parishes, and there were some cities, such as Stuttgart and those on the Ruhr which had a somewhat more pious reputation than the others. Thus in Saxony in 1876 there was a clear progression from 'real peasant villages', where weekly church attendance was 20–40 per cent of the Protestant population, through villages with large estates, and administrative centres, to the great cities, where it was around 5 per cent, to small industrial towns, where it sometimes dropped to 1 per cent. In fact, as the relatively low attendance in estate villages and those with a large industrial population suggests, the real division was not between town and countryside, but between the one social group that remained strongly attached to the church (the peasants), and those social groups that were most detached from the church (labourers, factory operatives, and the professional and business classes). Also, the fact that social composition, rather than density of population was the most important factor in determining the religiosity of a town is suggested by the fact that attendance was higher in Leipzig or Dresden than in many of the more homogeneously working-class communities in the surrounding area.[15]

In England the contrast between town and countryside was less sharp, and the primary importance of class was more obvious. At the religious census of 1851 the median ratio of attendance to population was 64·8 per cent in rural areas of English counties, and 49·6 per cent in the towns. In both town and countryside the non-church-goers came mainly from the working-class population, and middle-class church attendance remained high until the end of the century. Therefore references to the 'religious problems' of the cities really meant those of the working-class districts of the cities, and though the Anglican clergy sometimes complained of middle-class alienation from the established church, no one suggested that such people were generally irreligious – most would be Nonconformists. In so far as there was a specifically urban religious problem in England it lay in the fact that urban labourers and craftsmen were probably more likely to be religiously indifferent and certainly were often attracted to secularism than those in the countryside.

In France the church was weak in many of the great cities, notably Paris, and if national church attendance statistics had been available, they would certainly have shown a higher average in country than in town. But the difference between town and country was less significant than those between social classes and between regions. In the first half of the century the class most alienated from the church was the bourgeoisie; in the second half it was the working class. And throughout the century there were marked regional contrasts: in the 'dechristianised' zones of the centre, religious practice was low both in rural areas and in the towns; in the Catholic regions, such as Alsace-Lorraine and the extreme north, the peasantry was overwhelmingly practising, and the church was also fairly strong in the industrial areas.

IV

The years of the Revolution in France frequently saw 'patriot' towns pitted against a counter-revolutionary, or simply an indifferent country-side. Indeed Tilly explains the response to the Revolution in the west largely in terms of varying degrees of urbanisation. The main reason for this contrast was the concentration in the towns of those middle-class occupational groups that provided the most consistent supporters of the 'patriot' cause. But it was also in the towns that a mass of newspapers and political clubs grew up which spread the ideas of the Revolution to many of the artisans, and superseded the parish-focused life of many rural areas.[16] In the early decades of the nineteenth century it was the bourgeoisie who remained the main enemies of the church and kept alive the reputation of the towns for irreligion. So for instance, in Catholic Brittany the towns of Brest and Lorient were isolated anti-clerical and liberal strongholds. Yet the fact that the real distinction was less between town and country than between classes was demonstrated by the fact that within the town of Brest there was a sharp distinction between the French-speaking bourgeois quarters on the left bank of the river Penfeld, 'Nineveh and Babylon' to the surrounding peasantry, and the popular quarters on the right bank, where half the population spoke Breton, the clergy still enjoyed a great following in the 1840s, and the people ended the day 'picking rosary beads and saying Paternosters by the thin light of a candle'.[17]

In England, on the other hand, anti-clericalism and secularism were mainly supported by craftsmen and small traders. Once again the class division was more important than that between town and country. In

London the irreligion of many workers contrasted with the piety of most of the middle and upper classes; meanwhile artisan radicalism was winning recruits not only in the few large towns but in the Pennine weaving villages.

If the bourgeoisie, at least in such countries as France and Germany, often stayed away from church, it was from lack of interest rather than lack of opportunity. In Frankfurt, for instance, they would rent a seat in church, and then not bother to sit in it. In the suburbs of the cities, however, partly because of the policies of bourgeois governments, great new working-class quarters were growing up with only the smallest provision for the religious needs of the population. In the later eighteenth century, in fact, there had still been a number of countries where the church seemed to be most deeply rooted in the towns. This was certainly true of Spain and Portugal, where many small and medium-sized towns were dominated by the church, and even the cities of Lisbon and Oporto had an extensive network of confraternities and of well-staffed parishes. On the other hand, in the rural south, parishes were very large and many people seldom saw a priest. As David Higgs comments: 'the migration into urban centres that was the consequence of the eighteenth-century demographic surge in Portugal as elsewhere, especially to Lisbon from the adjacent Estremadura and the Alentejo, brought non-practising country people into pious towns.' Even in France where a contrast between the piety of the countryside and the indifference of many townspeople was beginning to appear before the Revolution, a city like Paris had a very large active population of priests and nuns, and numerous chapels staffed by regular clergy to supplement the admittedly insufficient parish churches; and if the aristocracy and *grande bourgeoisie* tended to be luke-warm Catholics, many observers stressed the continuing piety of the poorer classes.[18]

But there is already evidence of what nineteenth-century Britain would term 'spiritual destitution' in the immigrant suburbs of some eighteenth-century towns. Hufton cites a suburb of Lodève with 2 priests for 5,000 people, and a settlement on the outskirts of Montpellier, with 1,500 people and no priest at all, both drawing their population from the pious Massif Central, and both with large numbers among their population who had lost touch with the church.[19] In the nineteenth century comments of this sort were to become general. In Brussels and Paris the relationship of urban growth to religious provision has been traced in considerable detail.[20] In Brussels the population increased from 67,000 to 611,000 between 1803 and 1900. During this time the number of parishes increased from 11 to 42, and the number of priests from 40 to 161. In other words, the average size of parish, and the number of people for each priest both more than doubled; in both cases the scale of Catholic provision deteriorated almost continuously through the century. In Paris the population rose from 546,000 in 1802 to 2,537,000 in 1896, while the number of parishes increased only from 39 to 69. In 1802 there had been about 1 priest for 1,600 people; whereas in 1906 the ratios were 1:3681 in the centre of the city; 1:5760 in the inner suburbs, and 1:4095 in the outer suburbs. In both cities the problems were worst in the poorer districts, where local funds for building churches and paying priests in addition to those provided by the state were unlikely to be available. The record for parish size seems to be held by Notre-Dame de Clignancourt, on the north side of Paris, which in 1906 had 121,634 people. Contemporaries sometimes argued, and historians have echoed them, that in these conditions, religious habits were broken. Cardinal Guibert, Archbishop of Paris, referring in 1873 to the shortage of churches in the new suburbs of the city, wrote: 'Baptised Christians live there, who have, at least in many cases, become strangers to religious habits, because parish churches are too far away or too few. They could be called a people without altars . . .'. While it is quite likely that many of these immigrants to Paris would not have gone to church even if there had been churches there, migrants to Brussels were drawn mainly from the highly Catholic villages of Flanders and Brabant, and Houtart's evidence suggests that the insufficiency of religious provision in the city may have been a significant factor in the breaking of the traditions they brought with them. Thus in 1849 the parish council of the Minimes church in the poorest area of Brussels opposed in the following terms a proposed extension of their boundaries, arguing at the same time that they really needed an extra church:

Distance from the church of the Minimes is for many inhabitants a cause, if not a pretext, for non-participation in divine worship. Besides, the church of Minimes is clearly too small to hold all the population of the parish. They cannot all find room there on saints' days, and some of them have to stand in the street during the service.

In 1853, the same body was asking for an additional priest, arguing that the present staff of clergy could not cope with the demands made on them. They wrote:

our catechisms are attended by 7–800 children each year; . . . more than 400 have been admitted to First Communion this year; . . . during the fortnight before Easter . . . the confessionals are assailed every evening by a crowd of workers, who keep our priests there until 11 o'clock or midnight; and rouse them at 4 the next morning; they also have to bring help and the consolations of religion to thousands of the sick and the infirm, especially when an epidemic has broken out in the capital, as these usually hit the poorest hardest, and our population is made up almost entirely of these. Add to that baptisms, burials and marriages . . .

In the best of circumstances the great flow of population into the towns in the nineteenth century would have required an enormous effort of fund-raising for the building of extra churches and the payment of extra priests. What needs to be stressed is that the state churches in the nineteenth century were not merely victims of uncontrollable forces, but that their failure to keep pace with the rising population was a consequence of human choices. Of these the most important were the policies of government. In France the first big blow to the urban parish network was struck by the Civil Constitution of 1790, which, in Paris, for instance, halved the number of parishes, and by the Concordat of 1801, which for the time being fixed the number of urban clergy that the state would support at a level far below that obtaining before the Revolution. From then until the Separation of Church and State the rhythms of urban church provision were determined by the priorities of successive governments. By the terms of the Concordat no new parish could be formed without government authorisation: under a pro-clerical regime like the Second Empire, new parishes were formed, and funds were available to pay more clergy; under the First Empire, the July Monarchy and the Third Republic, authorisations were very seldom granted, and the church's budget was kept down. In Belgium, which shared the system established by Napoleon as a result of the Concordat, and has kept it ever since, governments unsympathetic to the Catholic church ruled for a large part of the nineteenth century; but with the entry into power of the Catholic party in 1884 the climate changed, and from 1894 there was a big programme of church expansion in Brussels, which by 1947 had cut the average size of parish by more than a quarter, and improved the ratio of priests to people by a sixth, although the population had almost doubled in this time. In England the main obstacles to church expansion in the early nineteenth century seem to have been a combination of obstruction by vested interests, and the apathy of church leadership and government. Again the movement of reconstruction that got under way in the 1830s and 1840s never made good the ground that had been lost, but it showed what was possible when the will and the means existed. It would seem that in the nineteenth century it was the lack of will or, more frequently, the strength of the opposing forces, that hindered the churches' response to urban growth.

Even more important, however, than the weakness of the church machinery in the poorer districts of the cities was the growing rift between the working class and the rest of the urban population, and the development of a distinctive working class sub-culture, in terms of which the clergy appeared as unwelcome intruders. A classic example of this evolution is to be seen in such southern French cities as Marseille and Toulouse, which in the early nineteenth century were strongholds of Catholicism and Legitimism, and where in the second half of the century the working class became alienated from local political and religious traditions, abandoning the church and moving to the Left. In Toulouse this transition has been explained in terms of the change from an aristocrat-dominated local economy, in which social relations were based on patronage, to the impersonal relations of commercial and industrial capitalism, and the associated rise in class consciousness. In Marseille, where there was an enormous movement into the city of workers from Italy and from all over southern France, the change has been linked with the decline of the city's artisan culture, which had been integrated into that of the city as a whole, and of which Catholicism had been a part. In both cities the strength of Catholicism was associated with the strength of Legitimism, and both depended on the strength of ties crossing the lines of class; in both, popular Catholicism declined as Legitimism disappeared, and as class antagonism became the essential fact of economic and political life.

V

So in most parts of western Europe the nineteenth century, and the first half of the twentieth, saw the breakdown of religious unity in the cities. The result in most cases was neither any generalised irreligion, nor an anarchy of individually selected religious beliefs and customs, but a sharply differentiated pattern of habits and allegiances determined mainly by class or ethnicity.

In nineteenth-century, and even twentieth-century Europe, most city-dwellers have lived in fairly well-defined communities subject to a variety of informal controls. This has been most obvious at the top of the social hierarchy, where membership of an exclusive 'Society', embracing members of a national or local élite, has depended on some degree of accommodation to the fashions and norms of behaviour within it. So, for instance, an account of life in London's 'Upper Ten Thousand' in the 1880s reported that 'Society . . . holds in high esteem the Church as an institution and the ordinances of religion', and went on:

Most of the smart people go to church, to the Chapel Royal, or to St. Margaret's, Westminster, if they belong to the political set; and many other shrines are specially set apart for society's elect. Even those who do not go to church obligingly recognise in theory the obligation of going there when they talk of, or take part in, the after-church parade in Hyde Park.[21]

While the local rules might change, social pressures of this kind have always strongly affected the behaviour of those aspiring to membership of a self-conscious élite.

But at most other levels of urban life social pressures have continued powerfully to mould individual behaviour. A general phenomenon in nineteenth-century cities was a social segregation which sorted the population out into relatively homogeneous quarters. Neighbourhood pressures thus came increasingly to mean the pressures applied by social equals. The sense of neighbourhood tended to be especially strong in working-class areas, where until the introduction of cheap forms of public transport around the end of the nineteenth century, most travelling was done on foot, where it was often necessary to borrow money from neighbours or kin, or to obtain credit from familiar retailers, and where jobs often depended on personal contacts. The localisation of working-class life was a basic theme of Willmott and Young's *Family and Kinship in East London* (1957), though they believed that the pattern was then beginning to break up. A typical comment was that of a couple who had moved about ½ a mile across the Regent's Canal from Bow into Bethnal Green: 'In Bow you knew everybody, grew up with everybody, everybody recognised you. Over here they're a bit on the snobbish side – they know you're a stranger and treat you like one. They cater for you more in Bow. You like the place where you're mostly born, don't you?' A rather similar picture emerges from Robert Roberts's description of the part of Salford where he grew up in the early years of this century, a 'village' of thirty streets and alleys, 'perhaps as closed an urban society as any in Europe', or in an account of the working-class suburbs of Paris around 1950.[22]

In such tightly-knit communities social pressures severely limited the individual's freedom of action in most areas of life. In the 1830s church-going men had been subjected to charivaris in villages round Toulouse. In other villages public opinion operated equally brutally in the opposite direction: when in the 1880s and 1890s many village schools were secularised, the teachers appointed in place of the nuns sometimes found that none of the locals would sell them food. In the towns such uniformity of sentiment was never quite achieved. But towards the end of the nineteenth century there were still reports from several major cities of an anti-church feeling in the factories and workshops that was strong enough to make life quite uncomfortable for the church-going minority. In the west German textile centre of Barmen: 'There was at that time no section of society where it was harder to declare yourself a Christian than among the workers. Out of fear of their fellow men, and to escape the continual ridicule, many people gave up going to church.' In both Lille and London around that time it was said that working-class men who belonged to church organisations faced a good deal of sarcasm from some of their workmates.[23]

But though most urban-dwellers were governed by their own particular variety of conformism, it was still in the cities that new ideas could be heard, and that a dense network of deviant sub-cultures could support itself, and resist all the efforts of authority or the staid majority to control and suppress. Most general were the outcast sub-cultures of professional criminals and prostitutes, which dominated whole quarters in the great cities, and certainly made up quite a significant part of the total population. Other sub-cultures were based on sport and gambling, on distinctive sexual orientations, on political or religious sectarianism. In Britain one reflection of this cultural babel, right up to the Second World War, was the institution of park oratory, which did much to keep the city population entertained on Sundays, and also kept them in touch with a great range of ideas, most of them all too familiar, but some of them new. Field-preaching had been a key weapon of the evangelical revival in the eighteenth century, and had achieved its greatest success in the countryside; in the towns many alternative views of the world were available through the same medium. In the 1790s, when the evangelical movement was at its height and popular atheism was coming into the open for the first time, Londoners were being entertained for most of Sunday by 'field-disputations' between advocates of rival sects and between theists and atheists, with a break only for the ritual of Sunday dinner, which was sacred to all.[24] A century or more later much the same issues were still being debated each Sunday in such places as Victoria Park in the East End, Peckham Rye in south London, or Finsbury Park in the north, while the advocates of new creeds, from socialism to Confucianism, were also setting up their stands.

In Protestant countries this heterogeneity was reflected in the multiplicity of religious sects, many of them having a very small membership. Typical of urban England at the time of the religious census in 1851 was Bolton, where 85 per cent of worshippers were Anglicans, Wesleyans, Independents or Roman Catholics, but there were also three other varieties of Methodism, Baptists, Presbyterians, Unitarians, Quakers, Brethren, Swedenborgians, Mormons, and two congregations of unspecified denomination. A fairly similar denominational range was found in most other Lancashire towns, with the addition of Greek Orthodox in Manchester, Sandemanians and four branches of Presbyterianism in

Liverpool, Moravians in Ashton, Lady Huntingdon's Connexion in Oldham, Inghamites in Burnley, Southcottians in Warrington, Scotch Baptists in Preston, and also several Jewish congregations. All but two of these groups, as well as several others, were found in one part or another of London. By contrast, many rural districts were dominated by the Church of England; and where there was a significant number of Dissenters, they were often heavily concentrated in a single denomination. In recent years the church-going population in the towns has dropped, but the range of religious groups existing has become even wider. A survey of a mainly white suburb of Birmingham with a population of 20,000 in the early 1960s found that while 65 per cent of church-goers attended the Anglican or Roman Catholic church, there were 15 other congregations of 11 different Christian denominations. In the more heterogeneous environment of Handsworth, a population of 60,000 in 1973 supported more than 60 different religious congregations, including not only those of Hindus, Sikhs and Muslims, and of the major Christian denominations, but several independent evangelical churches, numerous varieties of Pentecostalism, Adventists, Children of God, Ras Tafarians, Spiritualists, and the Divine Light Mission.[25]

In the town, as in the country, the majority of the population have continued throughout this period to remain members of the church of their ancestors. While religious apathy tended to develop fastest in the towns, and to become the dominant characteristic of many of them by the early twentieth century, another important qualitative change associated with urbanisation was the increasing prominence in the organised religious life of small communities whose teachings and life-style set them in one direction or another sharply at odds with the norms prevalent in the wider society.

Nonetheless, it is possible to argue that the growth of great cities in itself weakened the influence of religion by providing the conditions in which a mass of new institutions could take over most of the functions formerly fulfilled by the church. As a study of Chicago in the 1930s and 1940s suggested:

The most important factor in weakening the influence of the churches is the centripetal pull of the urban milieu. There is a bewildering diversity of denominations and of types of churches within a denomination. The movies, ball games, social clubs and policy stations [illegal betting agencies] offer competing forms of participation, and throw doubt on all absolute conceptions of sin. The group controls of the small town are absent. The prosperous 'wicked' are a perpetual challenge to the 'poor saints'. 'Take the whole world and give me Jesus' may be the essence of the old-time religion. 'What do I get out of it?' is Bronzeville's persistent query.[26]

Similarly one could point to the proliferation of drinking places in nineteenth-century cities, to the beginnings of the leisure industry, represented first by cheap theatres and music-halls, or by skittle-alleys, and from the end of the century by the development of professional sport. Equally the multitude of political organisations and social clubs potentially replaced the church in many of its social functions.

Germany would seem to provide a good example of such a pattern. Here the *Vereine*, which originated in such cities as Hamburg and Basel in the late eighteenth century provided many of the bourgeoisie with a kind of alternative church – a place to meet with like-minded souls on Sundays, where ideals valid in all other areas of life were propagated, and a sense of common belonging was stimulated. In most of the cities the Sunday as a day of general rest and religion had by the 1830s and 1840s little reality. In the hours of worship on Sunday morning shops were open, the bars were doing a flourishing trade and bands were playing in the parks. In the later years of the century rural pastors were complaining of the large contingents of town-dwellers who descended on their parishes on Sundays to disturb the peace, and sometimes to mock the church-goers.[27]

On the other hand, this picture would not fit the British evidence before the twentieth century. The law kept the 'British Sunday' in operation right through the nineteenth century and well into the twentieth; and though the law was not entirely effective in working-class districts, in middle class districts it was assisted by the weight of public opinion at least until the 1890s. Because of the close link between religion and party politics, political parties tended to reinforce church loyalties rather than becoming rivals to them. Churches played a considerable part in the provision of cheap entertainment. And though nothing could compete on equal terms with the pubs as far as working-class males were concerned there was little difference in this respect between town and country. In Britain it would appear that the development of an all-absorbing leisure-world was more a consequence than a cause of the decline of the churches.[28]

VI

But perhaps the biggest change in the social role of religion that urbanisation and industrialisation have brought about is that the majority of people no longer need to seek supernatural aid during their working lives. A largely mechanised economy dependent on humanly controllable factors no longer requires prayers for rain. Scientific medicine and improved diet have also made less necessary the appeal to supernatural relief from sickness. Progress has not so much produced a race of rationalists as reduced the number of occasions when no human remedy is available The miracle-working saint or the faith-healer is no longer the first resort of the afflicted, but he or she is often the last resort. Zola in the 1890s described the 'white trains' which carried the sick and volunteer nurses to Lourdes: 'moving hospitals for the hopelessly ill, the drive of human suffering towards the hope of a cure, a furious need of relief;' by 1970 the number of visitors to the shrine would reach 3 million a year.[29] In many a church tucked away in the back streets of a great city a statue of Mary or the relic of a saint was a place of miracles, visited by cripples, by the mothers of soldiers, or the wives of drunkards. Perhaps the contempt of the Protestant churches for such 'superstitions' was one reason for their inability to attract the poor and uneducated. Certainly faith-healing has generally been a major attraction of the Pentecostal churches, which have won a following in most parts of working-class Europe during this century (though not the mass membership that they have in the cities of Brazil and Chile).

Moreover, there are two other vast areas of human need in which science can offer no help, and supernatural remedies of one sort or another inevitably have a monopoly: the desire to know the future, and to maintain contact with loved ones after they have died. If the Catholic church and certain branches of fundamentalist Protestantism derive widespread popular support from their claim to be able to offer possibilities of supernatural healing, those who claim to foresee the future or provide the means of communication with the dead usually operate on the margins of the Christian churches or outside them altogether. The continuing strength of such beliefs and practices is therefore quite compatible with a decline in the influence of institutional Christianity: but it does call in question the assumption that the result has been any general secularisation or rationalisation.

In England the religious response to the First World War, for instance, seems to have been not the return to the churches that some had predicted, but a widespread interest in spiritualism among the many thousands of bereaved at home, and a mixture of fatalism and magic at the front. The latter was summed up by the comment of an army chaplain that 'the soldier has got religion: I am not so sure that he has got Christianity'; and the editor of a volume on *The Army and Religion* summarised the evidence of his informants as follows: 'that the men who had been in the trenches had experienced an awakening of the primitive religious convictions – God, Prayer, Immortality – but that they did not associate these with Jesus Christ, that their thought of God was not Christianised'. Thus, it was said that men would pray before battle, and give thanks after, and that those who never took Holy Communion elsewhere did so at the front in the belief that it would stop them being hit; to make extra sure, they might carry a Bible as a talisman and they would keep their spirits up by singing hymns before battle (though in more relaxed circumstances they preferred to set obscene words to the well-known tunes). But this grasping for supernatural help implied no acceptance of the regime of moral discipline and formal religious observances encouraged by their chaplains.[30]

If mediums naturally found the demand for their services booming in war-time, scattered references suggest that their role in the day to day life of cities is probably greater than is usually recognised. For instance a series on German city life published about 1905 included a volume on spiritualism which generally emphasised the more exotic aspects of the subject, but also referred to the 'consultations' held every afternoon by 'Frau L., a cheerful lower middle class woman' with a reputation as a medium, whose husband, a Berlin carpenter, 'now lives from her earnings'. At these sessions she listened to the 'special sorrows' of 'the servant-girls of the neighbourhood, lovelorn shopgirls, mourning widows, anxious mothers, and now and then a representative of the male sex', and provided answers. In the evenings she held seances in which departed spirits conveyed messages to her while she was in a trance, and an audience of aristocrats, army officers and their wives, professors and the wives of big businessmen looked on. Hans Freimark, the author of the volume, stressed the general interest in all branches of the occult in the Germany of the time, the wide repute of certain mediums, and the numerous psychic societies. In the 1950s a Catholic 'religious sociologist' noted in passing the 'superstitions' prevalent in a working-class district of Lyon:

One is sometimes surprised to find a constellation of superstitions still very much alive in our rationalist and liberal cities – in the 20th century: What working class woman would pass under a ladder, would dare to light three cigarettes with the same match, offer a knife as a present, step on a spider in the evening, see one in the morning without trembling, knock over a salt-cellar without going through a propitiatory ritual, sit thirteenth at table? Others would be afraid to open an umbrella indoors, to marry in May (a growing superstition), to have dreamt of a child (signifying trouble), while some people think they were lucky to have met a hearse. How many women tremble as they read the weekly horoscope, and how many go to consult fortune-tellers, card-readers, and clairvoyants?[31]

Just *how* widespread these forms of non-Christian supernaturalism are in industrialised west-European societies, and how big a part they play in individual lives, is largely a matter of guesswork. One attempt was made by Geoffrey Gorer, on the basis of a questionnaire completed by readers of *The People* in 1951. He concluded from their answers that about a quarter of the English population 'holds a view of the universe which can most properly be described as magical; the future is for them pre-determined and knowable by various techniques which are not connected with either science or religion.' A more intensive study based on interviews in north London in the 1960s suggested that 18 per cent of those interviewed were 'very superstitious', working-class women scoring most highly in this respect, with those most prone to reject the 'superstitions' discussed being the mainly middle-class group of regular church-goers and the mainly male group of those with no religion. Among the forms of 'superstition' investigated by the authors were: practices intended to bring luck or avert bad luck, such as wearing charms; 'quasi-scientific' methods of knowing the future or communicating with the dead; and belief in fate. Each of these were practised or believed by about 20 per cent of those interviewed, and 18 per cent had actually visited a fortune-teller or astrologer.[32]

In the multitude of individual crises it is clear that large numbers of people in urban-industrial societies have continued to call for supernatural aid. But the collective turning to God, which had been so characteristic of the common response to crisis in past centuries was still not dead in the wars and foreign occupations of the 1940s. Dietrich Bonhöffer, in his famous letter from prison of 30 April 1944 stated that 'we are proceeding towards a time of no religion at all', and mentioned as an illustration the fact that 'this war, unlike any of those before it, is not calling forth any "religious" reaction'.[33] But whether or not Bonhöffer's observation holds for Germany, some of the occupied countries *did* undergo some sort of religious revival during the Second World War. The most striking example was the Soviet Union, where Christianity had been severely persecuted in the 1930s. But from occupied France too there were reports strangely reminiscent of those from the cholera-bound Black Country in 1849. Many *curés* reported a big increase in the number of Easter communicants in 1940. As one Pas-de-Calais priest told his bishop: 'In this parish where there used to be few church-goers, religion has now become in vogue.' At the other end of the war the *curé* of a nearby parish noted a drop in 1945: 'Like everywhere it's a devotion born of fear. The greater the dangers, the stronger the parochial life. When the bombardments were on, more people came to mass and to the rosary.'[34] However, the fact that the war years brought religious revival in occupied France and Russia, but not in Germany, suggests that it was not only a product of fear, but also of a process seen in a number of totalitarian countries in recent years by which the church takes on a new importance as the only sphere in which some degree of independence from an oppressive environment can be expressed. In the war years this was most strikingly seen in Norway, where the Lutheran church was the most important organiser of resistance to the Nazis, and briefly succeeded in transcending social divisions in a way that it has not done since, and had not done for many years before. Indeed Germany itself saw a religious revival in the years of famine and foreign rule in the later 1940s – a time of relief and hope for the rest of Europe, but for many Germans the grimmest they had ever experienced.

6 The Urban Middle Class

I

In 1882 Friedrich Nietzsche, descendant of a long line of Saxon pastors, first made his famous announcement that 'God is dead'.[1] Four years later he provided some sociographic detail. He wrote that religious indifference was typical 'of the great majority of German Protestants in the middle classes, especially in the great industrious centres of trade and traffic', and of 'the great majority of industrious scholars and the whole university population': 'They are no enemies of religious customs; if these are required, for instance by the state, they do what is needed, as one does so many things – with a patient and modest earnestness and without much curiosity or unease.'[2]

Protestant clergymen came to similar conclusions about the general picture, even if they would have rejected Nietzsche's glosses. A study of Saxony at the beginning of the twentieth century suggested that the professional and commercial middle class of the cities had been unchurched since the time of the Enlightenment, and a study of Württemberg referred to the religious 'indifference' of the middle class, with its 'democratic ideals, and freethinking ideas inspired by modern knowledge'. The latter book confirmed Nietzsche's comments on the academic community, referring to Tübingen as being 'like most university towns, not very church-oriented' – and indeed, a bad influence on the surrounding district. Historians have tended to come to similar conclusions. The educated middle class in Berlin was, it seems, already fairly detached from the church in the 1830s and 1840s: 'They belonged to the church, but each person made up his own religion. For the practical man, the church was an acceptable form of external display, especially for family celebrations.' By the 1860s and 1870s, while there were still few middle-class Protestants who actually left the church, the repudiation of church authority seemed to have gone a good deal further – the 'scientific world-view' was widespread, and the stubborn theological conservatism of many clergymen was a subject for ridicule.[3]

There seemed good grounds for suggesting that a combination of economic and social changes, political circumstances, and intellectual progress had resulted in the fact that God was indeed 'dead' for the educated city-dweller of Protestant Germany. As far as intellectual progress was concerned, the eighteenth century's relativisation of Christianity had culminated in the German universities during the 1830s and 1840s in the most concentrated attack on existing orthodoxy in the modern history of the faith. Of the most fundamental importance were the beginnings of the attempt to subject the scriptures to scientific historical investigation. Of greater immediate effect were Feuerbach's interpretation of religion in purely symbolic terms, on the basis of an assumed materialism, and above all Strauss's *Life of Jesus*, which intended to give the nineteenth century a Christ in which it could believe (by presenting the miraculous elements in the gospels as the expression of religious truths in mythical terms), but which seems to have had the effect of turning many readers into complete religious sceptics. Marx was thus able to claim in 1844 that 'the criticism of religion is now complete'. In the second half of the century there was an enormous market in Germany for books that popularised recent scientific developments, presenting them in a materialist and evolutionary framework. The most famous examples were Büchner's *Force and Matter* (1855) and Haeckel's *Riddle of the Universe* (1899), both of which assumed that there was an age-long *Conflict between Science and Religion*, to quote the title of J.W. Draper's equally famous polemic published in New York in 1874. Writers like Haeckel established the mental categories of large numbers of middle-class Germans (as also of many Social Democrats) in the later nineteenth century. But unless too large a part in the killing of God be attributed to the scientific polemicists, or to the theological radicals, it should be noted that Feuerbach assumed that supernaturalism was *already* dead, and that his task was to formulate a faith that could take its place.

It may be, therefore, that the real cause of the 'death of God' was to be found in the impersonal forces making for the rationalisation of life, the principle expounded by Max Weber. Weber defined the 'intellectualist rationalisation, created by science and by scientifically oriented technology' in the following terms:

it means that principally there are no mysterious incalculable forces that come into play, but rather that one can in principle master all things by calculation. This means that the world is disenchanted. One need no longer have recourse to magic or implore the spirits, as did the savage, for whom such mysterious powers existed.[4]

From this point of view, the decline of the supernatural was a long drawn out and very gradual process, but the nineteenth century, with its railways and its steamships, its electric telegraph and its huge mechanised factories, its universal education and its daily newspapers, perhaps administered the *coup de grace*. A parallel approach would be to follow up the observation of the American economist Simon Patten who, in 1912, attributed the moral turmoil in contemporary America to the fact that the country was passing from a 'pain or deficit' economy to a 'pleasure or surplus economy', and that religiously-sanctioned moral restrictions that had been appropriate to harsher times now seemed an unnecessary burden.[5] This change has been documented in the case of the merchant élite of Barmen who, in the early nineteenth century, when the local textile industry was based on domestic production, tended to cultivate close personal relationships with 'their' workers, to exercise both a paternal authority over them and a paternal interest in their well-being, to worship with them in the same Calvinist churches, and to take on positions of responsibility in town and parish. However, as production began to be concentrated in large bureaucratically-run factories from around the 1850s and 1860s, the élite moved out of the town into suburban villas, they began to adopt a more ostentatious life-style, they applied themselves more seriously to 'enjoying' their wealth, they ceased to take much part in church affairs or in town government, and by the end of the century they were giving up going to church altogether. As far as the general middle-class city population is concerned the nineteenth century saw the development of a large apparatus of commercial leisure provision and of secular, class-specific social clubs and recreational organisations.

The other sort of factor that has to be considered in explaining middle-class irreligion is the widespread alienation for political reasons from the Protestant church. In Prussia, at least, state control of the church was systematically used, especially after 1819, to ensure that conservative clergy were given preferment, and that the many pastors and theologians who were politically liberal were harassed, and where possible, dismissed. The alliance between aristocratic conservatives and the Pietist movement that developed in Prussia during these years also meant that theological liberals were *ipso facto* suspect, whether or not they were politically active. One result of this was considerable middle-class support for the Halle-based Friends of Light movement in the 1840s, organised by clergymen and theologians, and directed towards liberalisation of the Prussian state and greater theological freedom in the church. But this movement was fairly rapidly squashed by state and church authorities, and many of its leaders were ousted from their parishes or their chairs. After the defeat of the revolutions of 1848–9, when the Protestant clergy had generally supported the forces of reaction, liberals tended to lose all faith in the church. The breach was confirmed in the 1850s, when in Prussia the conservative stranglehold over the church became complete, and religion was deliberately used by the authorities in many parts of Germany as an agent of 'restoration'. The fact that the retraction of many of the constitutions granted in the year of revolution went hand in hand with measures to increase the amount of religious teaching in the schools and to enforce a stricter observance of 'Sunday rest' naturally did nothing to increase the loyalty of Protestant liberals towards their church. The alliance between the Protestant church and political conservatism lasted until 1945: though there continued to be a minority of liberals, and later socialists among the clergy, they were heavily outnumbered, and at times directly attacked by the church authorities.

The importance of the political factor becomes clear when we look at the highly differentiated social profile of German urban Protestantism. Though women were generally more involved than men in church life, there were also considerable differences between the religious tendencies of the various occupational groups. While the working class and the professional and commercial middle class were the most secularised sections of the population, aristocrats, higher officials, and the lower middle class were much more church-oriented. Thus in Dresden many aristocrats were active in lay Protestant organisations, and in Berlin the best attended parish church was the fashionable (and theologically conservative) Matthäikirche in the Tiergarten area. But the mainstay of most city parishes seems to have been the 'little men' (*die kleinen Leute*): self-employed craftsmen, minor officials, clerks.[6] This group seems to have hung on to its inherited Protestant culture, when both working class and bourgeoisie were tending to abandon it. A study of German lower-middle-class culture between about 1750 and 1850 noted the great preponderance of religious books in inventories of books possessed by members of this group; it went on to suggest that 'the religious-moral world of edification and devotion can still be termed the spiritual home of the German lower middle class in the nineteenth century', and that a 'home-based piety', which was also found in other classes, had its 'prototype' in the petite bourgeoisie.[7] In Barmen, for instance, where the lower middle class seems to have had a particularly strong sense of group identity in the later nineteenth century, it was distinguished by religious orthodoxy, patriotism, political conservatism, hard work, thrift, and a passion for cleanliness. It might be suggested that the faith of the small producer or trader was preserved by limited education and work in a one-man shop, both tending to insulate him from new ideas. But the fact that aristocrats, with their relatively high levels of education, and clerks and officials, employed in large offices, were also relatively devout suggests that political factors were important in determining which sorts of ideas those in a given social group were willing to listen to. Nonetheless it is true that levels of religious practice were so low in many German cities that the differences within the urban population seemed of minor importance: there seemed to be a clear contrast between the secularisation of the cities and the piety of many peasant populations. For instance, statistics of communions by members of the Protestant state churches in the years 1891–5 show Berlin and the three overwhelmingly urban churches of Lübeck, Bremen and Hamburg bottom of the list, Hamburg being bottom of all, with 10 communions per 100 Protestant church members, as against 80 in Schaumburg-Lippe, which came top.[8] It is also worth noting that the 'educated' middle class, whose liberal politics tended to alienate them from the state churches, showed little inclination to support the Protestant sects either: these found their supporters in the lower middle class and, to a lesser extent, the working class.

However, there was no corresponding degree of secularisation during the nineteenth century in the mainly Catholic areas of southern and western Germany. Comparison with France and Britain provides further evidence of the complexity and variability of middle-class religious patterns, and suggests that the religious consequences of the economic and intellectual revolutions of the nineteenth century were substantially determined by the nature of the political context within which they operated.

II

Asa Briggs has identified the years 1780–1846, and more especially the period of the French wars, as the time in which a 'middle class consciousness' developed in English politics.[9] For the French bourgeoisie, 1789 and the years immediately following obviously had a similar formative influence. But it is clear that the religious component of this middle-class consciousness was strikingly different in France and in Britain. In France the most important religious reference-point for the bourgeoisie was the eighteenth-century Enlightenment; in England or Scotland it was more likely to be the evangelical revival. In Britain a fusion of the values of the middle class and of evangelical Protestantism took place, which powerfully influenced both church life and the general life of the middle class throughout the century. In France there were some areas, notably the northern textile region, where the industrial bourgeoisie had a strongly Catholic stamp, but in general the bourgeois mentality was rationalist, and the Catholic church was seen as the preserve of aristocrats and the uneducated.

In many parts of France the events of the 1790s led to the crystallisation of an attitude of hostility to the church, framed in terms of eighteenth-century rationalism, in wide circles of the bourgeoisie. After 1815 the paths of the church and of the liberal bourgeoisie only diverged further, as the church identified itself firmly with Legitimism, and as Ultramontanism, with its combination of papalism and anti-rationalism began to gain a hold over the clergy. In the years of Empire and Restoration 'Voltairian' was the word most commonly used to describe the bourgeois approach to religion. In the highly Catholic Breton *département* of Morbihan, for instance, the town of Lorient was 'a world apart', where the Prefect commented in 1814 that: 'The bourgeois are *philosophes* and will never blush to be so,' (and indeed, in the episcopal city of Vannes, when a leading citizen went bankrupt in 1817, an inventory of his library revealed seventy-two books by Voltaire and thirty-seven by Rousseau.)[10]

During the years of the Restoration and the July Monarchy Cholvy reports a 'pronounced detachment from the church on the part of the *notables*, and especially of the *petits bourgeois* of the villages and small towns', in the greater part of the Montpellier diocese. Lawyers, judges, doctors, retired officers were among those frequently mentioned by the clergy as exercising an unfavourable influence in their parishes. Daumard defines the Parisian bourgeois of the years 1815–1848 as 'the rationalist city-dweller': peasants were totally alien to him, and God, though not dead, was very remote. The leitmotiv of the bourgeois view of the world was the belief in the reality of choice, and the possibility of dominating circumstances. The lack of interest in the Catholic faith was reflected in the lack of religious objects in houses or pious references in wills, in the fact that few bourgeois became priests or nuns, or left money for religious purposes.[11] However, such comments about the attitudes of the class as a whole referred mainly to adult males: women were certainly much more frequent attenders at church, however lukewarm their faith may have been. The leading practitioners of anti-clerical rowdyism were young males: whenever in the 1820s a mock mass was held, a mission or a procession disrupted, the odds were that students of law or medicine, or other middle-class youths, were the leaders, and in the 1830s it was they who took the lead in pulling down the gigantic mission crosses erected under the Restoration – sometimes in the face of fierce popular resistance.

The common factor uniting the various forms of bourgeois opposition to the church was anti-clericalism – suspicion of the power and pretensions of the priests, and especially their association with reactionary politics. But the positive content of this bourgeois religion or irreligion varied a good deal. One area of contention was the acquisition of church lands by many bourgeois during the Revolution, and the attempts by some of the clergy after the Restoration to obtain the return of those lands to the church. A widely accepted position was that of those bourgeois spokesmen who, without rejecting Christianity or religion as such, opposed the slogans of 'liberty', 'progress' and 'enlightenment' to the 'despotism' and 'superstition' of the clergy. Typical was a paper like *L'Echo des Alpes* published in Grenoble from 1819 to 1821, the constant theme of which was that 'the intolerance of the priests will bring down the Catholic religion'. *L' Echo* was strongly critical of bishops who issued militant pastorals denouncing the age, and it specialised in exposés of priests who refuse to bury suicides, denounced unmarried mothers from the pulpit, stopped public dancing, or formed close links with local aristocrats. Instead it offered a non-dogmatic ethical Christianity, reminiscent of Rousseau, and of some sections of the constitutional church – and indeed one that probably continued to find influential exponents in some of the surviving juring priests. As Poulat points out, rebels against the Catholic church in nineteenth-century France often saw themselves as exponents of a more authentic Christianity, in revolt against the degenerate form of the faith then in the ascendant.[12] There certainly were, however, bourgeois anti-clericals who were convinced deists or atheists. Probably a large proportion of them were Freemasons. Already in the beginning of the nineteenth century the lodges of the Morbihan have been described by an historian as a 'counter-church'. At Vannes, during the First Empire, all the leading officials were members of the masonic lodge, and the same group found itself in repeated conflict with the bishop and clergy.

The large part played by political factors in determining the religious position of the bourgeoisie is strongly suggested by the 'return to the church' of a large section of this class, which became marked during the Second Empire, though in some places the first indications of this trend had come in the 1830s and 1840s. The decisive period was the political crisis of 1848–51, ending with the victory of the 'party of order', in which aristocracy, grande bourgeoisie and most of the clergy made common cause under the leadership of Louis Napoleon. A vivid reflection of the mood of these years appears in a letter written in November 1848 by a Parisian priest, the *abbé* Maillard, to the bishop of Autun:

As for what is now called *la classe bourgeoise*, so hostile to the church before February, I do not really think it has changed its mind, but the memory of the archbishop's devotion has made an impression; and then it is afraid. . . . A month ago I was with several industrialists and proprietors, each more concerned than the others to discredit the systems of Proudhon, Cabet . . ., but none of them much concerned (I knew them) with God and the Gospel. There was a discussion on socialism and communism, and, inevitably, communism and socialism were soon borne down by an avalanche of serious or humorous arguments. The right of property remained sole master of the field, and was proclaimed to universal applause *sacred, fundamental, inviolable*.

The priest remained silent and when questioned as to his attitude, he replied that there could be no secular basis for the law of private property, and that the only ground on which the poor could be persuaded to respect it was the belief that the law of God forbade 'theft', and that those who respected God's laws would be rewarded in another life.

'So according to you', asked with a preoccupied air, a big industrialist, owning a factory worth more than a million, '*without religion* property is no longer a right and Proudhon is right?' 'That's it.' . . . Since that time two of the company (including the industrialist) have come to find me, and have started discussions on religion, from which I expect, with God's grace, the best results. That is how things are with the bourgeoisie: it will help us as a counter-weight to doctrines that it fears, and as a kind of spiritual police, called to obtain respect for the laws which benefit it. But that is the limit of its esteem and confidence in us.[13]

Local studies have reported a similar trend in many other parts of France. In Orléans the *grande bourgeoisie* were all liberals and 'Voltairians' before 1848. After that they were divided, but those who 'rallied' to Napoleon III generally adopted a friendlier attitude to the church, and sent their children to schools providing religious education. In the Hérault 1848–51 seems to have marked a decisive turning-point: the definitive alienation from the church of many republicans, a return to the church of some *notables*, as an example of which Cholvy quotes one in nearby Nîmes who made his first communion in 1849 at the age of 61. In Lille there was a clear division in the later nineteenth century between a Catholic and a republican bourgeoisie – though in the 1890s they would co-operate against the socialist majority in the city council. In the Lille area many of the clergy enjoyed a close relationship with the bourgeoisie. In 1884 an 'Association of Catholic Employers of the Nord' was formed. Its members established chapels in their factories, with prayers at the start of the day's work, and a variety of confraternities and benefit organisations. In some instances membership of these was a condition of employment. The relationship between clergy and industrialists had advantages for both parties: the latter welcomed the church's attacks on socialism; and the former needed wealthy patrons in order to keep the vast machinery of Catholic enterprises in motion. But it was never as close as the relationship that had once existed between clergy and aristocracy. Following Leo XIII's encyclical *Rerum Novarum* (1891), a split developed between the majority of Catholic employers, who were ardent believers in economic liberalism, and those Social Catholics who argued for independent trade unions and the 'just wage'. With the powerful development of Catholic trade unions in the textile towns north of Lille in the early twentieth century, the economic role of Catholicism became even more ambivalent.

While one part of the French bourgeoisie was becoming more Catholic in the second half of the nineteenth century, the other was becoming more bitterly anti-clerical. In 1877 d'Alzon, founder of the Assumptionist order, wrote: 'France is becoming dechristianised day by day. By whom? By the doctors, the lawyers, the journalists, the schoolteachers, who have perverted the countryside.'[14] From the 1860s the middle and lower bourgeoisie were the leaders in opposition to the church. The aristocratic and upper-middle-class 'Voltairians' of earlier years had often feared to pass on the fruits of their enlightenment to the people, as they thought the masses needed the disciplines of religion: their petit-bourgeois successors of the later nineteenth century deliberately sought to democratise scepticism, believing that 'superstition' served only to keep the people miserable and the reactionaries in power.

III

In England and Scotland too the development of a self-conscious middle class in the early nineteenth century led to a widespread attack on the power and privileges of the established church. But the characteristic form of this revolt was religious Nonconformity. Consequently, while the nineteenth century was a period of intense sectarian conflict, often reflecting the antagonism between the land-owning class and its enemies, there was also a certain degree of moral and religious consensus within the middle and upper classes of nineteenth-century Britain based on a common Protestantism, most commonly of evangelical cast. The middle class, and especially the upper middle class, was the group most affected by the religious revival of the early nineteenth century, and for several decades the attitudes and norms of behaviour within the middle class carried a strongly evangelical stamp. By the middle of the nineteenth century a pattern of normal middle-class behaviour had been established, which included at least external adherence to an evangelical Protestant way of life. The Tory journalist, J.W. Croker, referred in 1843 to:

the fuller attendance on every occasion of public worship and the multiplication of these occasions – the more willing adhesion to reverential forms – the more exact observance, both public and domestic of the Sabbath – the growing disfavour and discouragement of profane or even idle amusements – the spread, we had almost said the fashionable vogue, of religious literature, and the diffusion of – if we may venture to employ a metaphor on such an occasion – a kind of Christian tint over the general aspect of society.[15]

One area in which appearances, at least to some extent, belied reality was the continuing existence of a dual standard of sexual morality, though even here, Taine, who visited Britain in 1858 and 1862 and was strongly impressed by the religiosity of the middle and upper classes, felt that evangelical propaganda in favour of an equally strict standard for both sexes had had some effect.[16] It is not so clear at what point this normative middle-class religiosity became established. The famous reference in the *Annual Register* for 1798 to the lines of carriages outside the churches seems to have been among the first indications that a religious revival among the wealthy had begun. But for many years after that people were referring to the revival as a fairly recent phenomenon. That these norms of behaviour were maintained by powerful social pressures was strongly suggested by the comments of a French visitor to Britain in 1828, who wrote that: 'both in England and in Scotland I am convinced that religious observance has shown a marked increase among all classes in the last ten years'. He went on: 'Different people, merchants, lawyers, etc., confessed to me their real feelings, feelings they are forced to hide, for if they did not go to church they would be the butts of all the local gossips and they might have to face the unfortunate consequence of this.'[17]

Yet beneath the surface of religious conventionalism there were two quite different forms of religious revival at work. One was the equivalent of the aristocratic pietism of Prussia in the same years. Its strongholds were the nobility, gentry, and above all, the well established and conservative sections of the upper middle class; it was heavily Anglican and Tory; and like the equivalent movements on the continent it was strongly affected by the social fears of the 1790s. The other was predominantly Nonconformist. It identified the religious revival with the cause of social progress as understood by the liberal and radical middle class.

The conservative religious revival, at first strongly evangelical, later often High Anglican, was beginning to gather support in the 1780s, but it was not until after the turn of the century that a widespread change in the religious outlook of the ruling class became evident. By this time something very similar to the 'return to the church' in post 1848 France seemed to be underway. In Paris in 1848 the *Abbé* Maillard had told his worried bourgeois audience that deism was not enough, and only a thorough-going Catholicism would persuade the poor in a revolutionary age to accept their poverty. There is a similar contrast between Burke's

Reflections on the French Revolution (1790) with its assumption of an undogmatic and uncontroversial state religion, accepted by all reasonable men, and the manifesto of the new evangelicalism, Wilberforce's *A Practical View of the Prevailing Religious System* (1797), which argues that the continuing viability of a hierarchical social order requires a change of heart by both rich and poor, and the acceptance by both of the disciplines and the consolations of a highly dogmatic form of Christianity.[18] 1804 brought the first of several parliamentary grants for church-building, and throughout the first half of the century Anglican propaganda made heavy play with the claim that the church was the chief barrier against the forces of revolution. Of course it is difficult to discover how strongly such considerations weighed at the individual level. But they almost certainly had a major part in the development of a public opinion that favoured religious orthodoxy. For as Wilberforce's son, Henry, an Anglican clergyman later converted to Rome, wrote in 1838, many people who were not themselves very religious 'are naturally inclined to follow the general example of their equals, and they have children and servants they would gladly see governed by religious principles'. Or as Hook, vicar of Leeds from 1837 to 1859 wrote, there were many 'political Churchmen who uphold the Church merely or chiefly because it is established and forms part of the constitution of the country'.[19] There was thus a very large element of political calculation and social conformism in the revival of conservative religion, and much of its effects on individual belief and morality were superficial. But there was more to it than that. Conservative evangelicalism did have a profound effect on the prevailing mores of the middle and upper classes, and on the lives of many individual members of these groups.

Wilberforce, the leading evangelical Anglican around the end of the eighteenth century, was a country gentleman from a Hull merchant family; other leading laymen at this time included bankers, an East India merchant, civil servants, and a brewer. Typically they came from a well established upper-middle-class background. A large part of their beliefs was shared with evangelical Protestants at many other times and in many other social milieux. But they had a number of distinctive emphases: one was a stress on social hierarchy and on submission to authority; another was an obsessive sabbatarianism; above all there was an emphasis on the right stewardship of time. Wilberforce kept an exact tabulation of how much time he had spent each week under each of nine headings, one of which was time 'squandered'. Hannah More, the famous evangelical publicist, wrote a poem on 'Time' and another on 'Early Rising', which was also one of Wilberforce's preoccupations. 'Idleness' was a favourite term in the evangelical vocabulary and 'the annihilation of portions of time' a favourite concept. The evangelicalism of the Clapham Sect allowed an important section of the ruling class to rule with a good conscience, by persuading them that social hierarchy was divinely ordained, and by providing them with a set of principles which would enable them to rule with apparent justice; it also helped them to rule more efficiently, providing principles of regularity, self-discipline, and honest dealing that enabled evangelicals to prosper wherever these qualities could contribute to success.

If the religion of the Clapham sect was the evangelicalism of a highly conservative élite, there was also a more strictly middle-class evangelicalism of those who were on the way up, and whose criticism of existing society went some way beyond the attack on idleness and sabbath-breaking favoured by the Claphamites. Some of them were Anglicans, but most were Nonconformists; in Scotland the United Presbyterians and the Free Church met the needs of a similar constituency. In this mould were many newly rich manufacturers and medium-scale traders. They too always had an eye to the clock – like Sir Titus Salt (1803–76), the Bradford woollen manufacturer, M.P. for the city, philanthropist and Congregationalist, who 'when he made an engagement was punctual to the minute, and he expected the same in others who had dealings with him. . . . It was the same at home as at business; the hour of meals was observed with precision, and all other domestic arrangements were conducted on the same principle of order. With watch in hand he would await the time for evening prayers, and then the bell was rung instantly for the household to assemble.'[20] They too despised idleness, banned frivolous pleasures, and adhered to the strictest possible interpretation of the proper observance of Sunday. But the purpose and direction of their monumental self-discipline was different. Like Edward Baines, editor of the *Leeds Mercury* (a leading organ of political and economic liberalism) and progenitor of a long line of wealthy Congregationalists, they believed themselves to embody 'the spirit of improvement' and to be 'self-harnessed to the car of progress'. For men of this stamp industry and enterprise were the paths that everyone could and should take out of the 'station to which they had been called'; and education, far from being a mere instrument of educating the poor to accept subjection, had a quasi-religious significance as the great agent of emancipation. As Samuel Smiles, whose views were largely characteristic of this social stratum, wrote in 1845: 'education will teach those who suffer how to remove the causes of their sufferings; and it may also make them dissatisfied with an inferiority of social privilege. This, however, is one of the necessary conditions of human progress.' Smiles then went on to denounce those poor people who, he claimed, were '*contented* with their condition'.[21]

Nineteenth-century middle-class liberalism thus had a two-edged character: in theory and to some extent in practice too, it offered the masses
new possibilities of freedom and dignity; but by greatly exaggerating the
extent of these possibilities it re-inforced the self-admiration of the
successful minority, and gave the rich new reasons for despising the
poor. In so far as the rich tended, at least nominally, to be religious
people, and the poor were, for the most part, detached from the
churches, religion could easily get bound up with this scheme of
justification: the rich had got rich by dint of superior character, a product
of their religious faith, and the poor were poor, and deserved to remain
so, because they lacked these qualities. An extreme expression of this cast
of thought was the doubt expressed by an Aberdeen Church of Scotland
parish missionary in 1849 as to the genuineness of the conversion of those
recruits to the church who remained poor after joining the
congregation.[22]

An important part of nineteenth-century middle-class ideology in
Britain was the democratisation of the concept of respectability. In
eighteenth-century usage the term had been applied only to those who
merited respect by virtue of the property they owned. In nineteenth-
century usage it came to apply to those of whatever social status who
merited respect by virtue of their qualities of character. This 'character',
another important nineteenth-century concept, included such things as
industry, self-discipline, habits of order and cleanliness, and also a
concern for propriety.

After the period of acute class tensions in the first half of the
nineteenth century, a new form of paternalism was precariously established in many of the factory communities of Britain during the
prosperous 1850s and 1860s. It was part of the theory of this paternalism
that a genuine comradeship was possible between 'respectable' people of
different social classes on the basis of their common interests in the
prosperity of their firm, their membership of the local community, and
common participation in local institutions and movements. Characteristic figures of these years were the Quaker Palmers, owners of the
Huntley and Palmer biscuit firm in Reading from its small beginnings in
the 1840s until it became a limited liability company in 1898. One of the
three Palmer brothers was based in London; the other two lived in
Reading, close to the works, and remained leading figures in many areas
of the town's life until their deaths in the 1890s. George became mayor
and Liberal M.P. William Isaac, who formed a more intimate relationship with the firm's employees, was also actively involved in the town's
Mechanics' Institute, Temperance Society, Free Library, Liberal Party,
Sunday School Union, Gardening Association – and more besides.

This system was precarious because many workers were unattracted by the ideals of 'respectability'; because those who *were* 'respectable' were irked by the hierarchy and subordination inherent in even the most liberal form of paternalism; and above all, because it provided no cure to the continuing poverty of a large section of the population. But from about the 1850s to the 1880s it was a basic feature of life in many industrial areas, and social tensions were to some degree attenuated, or pushed beneath the surface. In this period church and chapel often provided the arena where 'respectable' employer and 'respectable' worker met on common ground. As Robert Moore says of the west Durham mining villages around the end of the nineteenth century, when a high proportion of union officials were Methodists, and several mine-owners were Methodists or Quakers: 'For the Methodists the worker-boss division may not have been the most relevant social division. . . .there were even some owners with whom the Methodist miners could have identified in terms of respectability: the owners were professing Christians; they were liberals, and they were patrons of good causes both locally and nationally.' In practice it is not entirely clear how much difference this affinity made. But certainly the two collieries owned by the Quaker Pease family, who were said to give preference to Methodists as employees, stood out from surrounding collieries because of the relatively harmonious relations between managers and the mainly Methodist union leadership. In the last quarter of the nineteenth century, the two sides were bound together by mutual respect, and common commitment to principles of negotiation and arbitration. Unfortunately for the Methodist miners they continued to adhere to these principles, which they regarded as practical Christianity, when the management was switching to more aggressive policies.[23]

IV

Pease and Partners became a limited liability company in 1898, and Moore traces from about that time a switch from 'personalised and paternal control of their workers towards more impersonal and calculative control'. Members of the Pease family continued to be connected with the company, but by the early twentieth century they had the life-style of country gentlemen, they were sending their sons to Eton, and they had left the Society of Friends. The same sort of evolution was transforming many other large companies and the families at the head of them at about the same time. In Reading Yeo identifies the 1890s as a crucial decade, with Huntley & Palmer's becoming a limited liability company, and two of the firm's founders dying. 'Both William Isaac and

George Palmer had bought land, but they were not country gentlemen in the sense that their successors became. There was a switch in the second generation from Quakerism to Anglicanism, from commercial education to public schools, from Liberalism to Conservatism (except for G.W.P.), from modest "provincial" town life, to extravagant metropolitan or country life, from refusing state honours to accepting them.' In the same decade the Social Democratic Federation began to establish itself in the town, and one of its leaders, Harry Quelch, told a meeting there in 1893 that 'all personal relationships between manufacturers and the employed had ceased, they were simply "hands" to make profits'. So one of the most distinctive forms of nineteenth-century middle-class Christianity was dying out: as employers adapted to the pressures of the market, and rejected the life of factory and community; while a growing body of their workers also repudiated the old ties.[24]

Thus in the late nineteenth century the economic framework for the ethos of puritanism and respectability was breaking down. In the large-scale bureaucratically run industrial combine characteristic of the new era, neither employer nor employed needed to impress the other with his moral credentials; religion was no longer needed as a common language, as personal communication between those at different ends of the economic hierarchy died out; and as the economic élite became divorced from the industrial community, they ceased to support local religious institutions with their time, or even their money. At the same time the importance of sectarian issues in politics was diminishing, and so was the importance of denominational allegiance as a basis for party. From the 1870s a polarisation of the electorate on class lines was underway, and from 1886 on many Nonconformists joined the general flight of the well to do from the Liberal ranks. As economic issues came to dominate politics, and as class began to override sectarian identity as a determinant of political allegiance, the church/chapel conflict lost much of its urgency; on the other hand, the fragmentation of British religious life, and the fact that the British labour movement never adopted the secularism of many continental socialist parties, made it difficult to use religion as a rallying-point for the conservative cause in the way that had been attempted in the early nineteenth century. (In any case, by this time, many of the Anglican clergy realised that any hopes they had of 'winning back' the working class depended on the church breaking its links with the Conservative Party.) So social and political conflict was ceasing to reinforce church loyalties.

In the last quarter of the nineteenth century, then, the economic and political circumstances that had determined the distinctive social role of religion for much of the century were disappearing. At the same time, the prevailing norms of middle-class morality and religious belief were under attack. These had been a product of the interpenetration of evangelical theology with an ethos of industry, self-discipline and achievement. From about 1875 the morality was beginning to be regarded by many middle-class people as irksome or even immoral, and the evangelicalism was being attacked both by those who wanted to liberalise theology, and by those who wanted to get rid of Christianity altogether.

Church attendance seems to have begun to drop in middle-class areas in the 1880s, and membership of Nonconformist denominations was failing to keep pace with the rise of population. A confusing variety of religious trends were making themselves felt. One was the tendency towards religious liberalism, foreshadowed by the Broad Church movement in Anglicanism around the middle of the century, but reaching its furthest development towards the end of the nineteenth century and the beginning of the twentieth in the Nonconformist chapels, especially those of the Congregationalists. From the late 1870s such evangelical cornerstones as the belief in the verbal inspiration of the Bible and the everlasting punishment of the wicked were under open attack. The liberal Protestants of these years tended to reject the evangelical gospel of individual salvation, and very often adopted what came to be called in the U.S.A. the 'social gospel', according to which Christians instead of saving individuals from a corrupt world, should primarily be concerned with the building of a just society. While some devout Christians kept their Protestantism but abandoned nearly all of the classic Reformation doctrines, others were retaining their orthodoxy, but abandoning their Protestantism, by becoming Anglo-Catholics, or occasionally by joining the Roman church. In the later years of the nineteenth century the Anglo-Catholics became the most dynamic section of the Church of England, growing fast in middle-class suburbs, and very active in working-class areas of the cities where, admittedly, the response was often fairly small.

The reasons for the increasing popularity in these years of Anglo-Catholicism were varied, and indeed contradictory. But one of the most important factors was a revulsion from the puritanism of the evangelicals, and the consequent desire for a religion which identified the holy with the beautiful, and saw the joys of life as gifts of God rather than temptations of the devil. Another tendency of these years was towards agnosticism, a term coined by T.H. Huxley in 1874, and one which provided an effective definition for the unbelief of many middle-class people who shrank from the strident atheism of Secularists like Charles Bradlaugh. In the 1890s middle-class agnostics were organised in the Ethical Societies, forerunners of the modern humanist movement, and the

Rationalist Press Association which published cheap editions of books critical of Christianity: the best known was a series called The Thinkers' Library which, besides numerous works of Charles Darwin, included many volumes on the theme of science versus religion, or attacking Christianity's social record. Agnosticism was itself a dogmatic position: it asserted that if there is a God he is unknowable. But more widespread, probably, than the confidence of those who transferred their faith from God to Science was confusion and doubt. In 1904 the *Daily Telegraph* published several thousand letters on the subject, 'Do We Believe?' The majority, apparently, answered, in some form or other, 'Yes', but there were also a great many correspondents who could offer no resounding certainties, one way or the other. The significance of the correspondence was twofold: it showed the widespread interest and the frequent anxiety that the subject of religious belief and doubt aroused; and it showed that doubt no longer needed to be suppressed, as for much of the nineteenth century it had been, but was now a subject that could be discussed openly.

But the greatest threat to the religious and moral consensus of mid-Victorian Britain lay in the revolt against the prevailing ethos of puritanism and self-restraint – a revolt that was fuelled not only by the desire for greater individual freedom, but also by disgust at the hypocrisy and the cult of appearances that this system often led to. The writers of the 1880s and 1890s attacked the prevailing norms of respectable behaviour with a ferocity probably unparalleled in European literature. In Sweden, according to a modern critic, the writers of the 1880s regarded prevailing values with 'a disgust amounting almost to nausea'.[25] In this respect British writers could scarcely match their German and Scandinavian contemporaries; but the homely sarcasm of Bernard Shaw may have been more effective than the bombast of Ibsen, Nietzsche or Wedekind. The leitmotiv of this literature was, as Bernard Shaw wrote, in explaining the anger that was aroused by Ibsen: the 'acceptance of the impulse towards greater freedom as sufficient ground for the repudiation of any customary duty, however sacred, that conflicts with it'.[26] One of the clearest expositions of the new moral thinking was an article of 1894 by the English journalist, Grant Allen, on 'The New Hedonism'. In this he declared that: 'Self-development is better than self-sacrifice'. And he went on: 'To be sound in wind and limb; to be healthy of body and mind; to be educated, to be emancipated, to be free, to be beautiful – these things are ends to which all should strain, and by attaining which all are happier in themselves and more useful to others. That is the central idea of the new hedonism.'[27] He was especially scornful of the downgrading of sexuality by the old 'asceticism'.

Writers like Allen were giving a logical form to the widespread discontent with existing morality. Few were yet ready for such an uncomprising rejection of old standards and assertion of new principles, but large numbers of middle-class people were moving gradually in the same direction. Even in those respectable chapel-going circles which Allen so much scorned, many of the old puritan taboos were being repudiated by the younger generation in the 1890s. It was a cliché of the time that Christianity must concern itself with 'the whole man', 'mind, body and soul'. More generally the old middle-class ethos based on restraint, self-discipline and an anxious concern with the requirements of respectability, was giving way to an ethic of self-fulfilment, that was based on the idea that every individual had a right to happiness, and that everyone had a right to seek it in his own way. A middle class which no longer had to establish its own distinct social identity was now intent on enjoying the prosperity earned by the labours and self-deprivations of the preceding generations. At this stage the most momentous practical change was the drop in the middle-class birth rate during the last quarter of the century, caused by the more widespread use of contraceptives.

Part of the same trend was the decline of the 'Victorian' Sunday. When Taine visited England in 1858 and 1862, the sabbath was still the great symbol of national piety, and one of the distinguishing peculiarities of English (and even more, of Scottish) life. By 1905, when the *Daily Telegraph* published a series of special reports on the English Sunday, it was in a state of limbo – no longer a day dominated by religion, but not yet fully given up to the cult of leisure, or to the sacred rituals of family life. Between about 1875 and 1885 dinner parties, trips into the country, boating, cycling, golf – all of them taboo from a strict evangelical view-point – began to take up the Sundays of the urban middle class. As the *Daily Telegraph's* report on Sunday in north London stated: 'the tendency among the middle classes is distinctly in favour of making Sunday more a day of innocent enjoyment than strict religion', and when in 1910 several Nonconformists in a middle-class suburb of London had written to the local paper, saying that they had ceased attending chapel because of the Radical partisanship of their ministers, another wrote saying:

It may be there are some whose whole or partial estrangement from their places of worship is due to their objection in this matter, but I fear that, as in my own case, so in most, the reason will be found in the allurements of the country, river, or sport, either for the sake of health, pleasure or both.[28]

Indeed a sports mania overtook a large part of the British middle class in the late nineteenth century; and though the religious were gripped by it as well as the irreligious, it seems that sport was becoming an alternative emotional focus for the lives of many of those who were losing interest in religion.[29] These years were extraordinarily rich in the organisation of old games and the invention of new ones. The enormous role of betting on horse races in working-class life during this period is well known; it may be that cycling, cricket, golf, tennis deserve an almost equally large part in any description of middle-class life.

V

So, by the time of the First World War, the middle classes of France and of Protestant Germany were deeply split in their approach to religion. In both countries religion and politics were closely related, and the more politically conservative sections of the middle class were those closest to the church; in both countries rationalist beliefs were fairly widespread, and those middle-class people who did not go to church were often strongly hostile; but whereas in Protestant Germany the most devout section of the urban population was the lower middle class, in France it was the wealthy middle class. In Britain the situation was rather different: in spite of the decline of middle class church-going from the very high levels prevailing in the mid-nineteenth century, militant irreligion was fairly rare; nor were there such wide differences between the various sections of the middle class, though in England, the lower middle class were more likely to be Nonconformists, and more likely to be non-church-goers. Most people kept some links with the churches, but interest in religion was declining, and there was a growing repudi-ation of the puritanical and restrictive aspects of religious ethics.

Nor would the picture have looked very different in the 1950s. Germany had been through the traumas of 1918, the Nazi period and rule by the occupying powers; at the end of it all the religious situation in West Germany had changed very little – in East Germany, admittedly, things were quite different. In France there was the same contrast between a Catholic middle class and an anti-clerical middle class, the same very marked class differentials in religious practice, the same regional contrasts. In Britain the gradual decline of the influence of the churches had continued, but still about a third of middle class adults were regular church-goers.

Evidence about middle-class religion in twentieth-century Britain is fragmentary and superficial: we know a fair amount about the numbers and social characteristics of church members, very little about their understanding of their religion – and we know even less about the religion of the many people who seldom go to church. Research in France and West Germany has gone rather deeper, and two studies of mainly middle-class parishes in Lyon and Hamburg undertaken in the 1950s and early 1960s show how varied the position of the churches in the major cities of western Europe still was.[30]

In the Lyon parish there were wide differences both between men and between women in the levels of religious practice. 57 per cent of professional men were practising Catholics, but only 10 per cent of male manual workers, the intermediate groups being (in descending order): middle managers, representatives and large-scale traders, white-collar workers, and shop-keepers. The Catholic bourgeoisie tended to come to mass in family groups – often very large groups, as practising women had twice as many children as the non-practising. They saw their church-going as a duty; but they also hoped to find in the church comfort, renewed strength, and answers to their personal religious problems. Their conception of the faith, the author suggested, was essentially individualistic, and some of them complained there was too much discussion of social issues and not enough dogma in the sermons. But the author of the study, Fr. Pin, stressed that Catholic practice and non-practice were collective phenomena. And since practising Catholics tended as a body to be more highly educated than the rest of the population, of higher social status, more often born in the city, and more likely to be registered to vote, he suggested that 'there is a close relationship between religious practice and integration into urban life'.

In Hamburg, however, Freytag was able to reverse this analysis. In his chosen parish only 2 per cent of Lutherans went to church in any given week (which was around the average for the city). He referred to these church-goers as a 'deviant' minority, and stressed their marginal charac-teristics (for instance, the high proportion of old people). As one interviewee said: 'Church-going has gone completely out of fashion. Previously one did not dare not go to church on Sundays. Today you're looked at if you do go.' (Actually you would have had to go some way back to find a time when church-going was the fashion in Hamburg.) The church was seen as a bureaucratic organisation, comparable to the state or the trade unions, taken for granted but evoking little emotional response. The conclusion was not that some alternative integrating institution had taken the place of the Lutheran church, but that in a pluralistic and highly complex society, where most people had lost faith in the possibility of significantly changing their environment, there was 'a loose co-existence of the most varied view-points in man's consciousness' and a tendency for each individual, or each family unit, to withdraw into its own private world. Thus few people had any firm dogmatic convic-tions, and only certain socially marginal groups found the church relevant to large areas of their life.

7 The Working Class

I

By the end of the nineteenth century the existence of a working class, with its sense of separate identity, its distinctive way of life, and its own severely harassed institutions, was a fact in every west-European country. Each city had its great proletarian zones, regarded with a mixture of fear, revulsion and fascination by the rest of the urban community. This distinctive way of life appeared to include a characteristic religious position: most workers were members of the church that was dominant in their own country, and most continued to celebrate with religious rites the great turning-points of life; but they seldom went to church at other times, and many of them regarded church and clergy with hostility. In Catholic and in Protestant countries, and in those with differing political institutions, similar stories were being told around 1900.

Typical was the situation in Sweden, where attendance at the Lutheran state church had fallen sharply in some working-class communities by the 1880s. The workers who gave up going to church and subsequently provided many of the pioneers of Social Democracy fell into two contrasted groups: the impoverished estate labourers, miners and brickmakers of the rural south, who suffered especially bad working conditions; and some relatively prosperous sections of the working class, including urban artisans and the Sundsvall saw-mill workers, who felt their superior position threatened by mechanisation. Around 1880 these groups were developing a strong sense of their own separate working-class identity. The commitment of the clergy to the principle of social hierarchy was resented, and 'the very presence of better-dressed persons from the higher and middle strata seems in culturally divided milieux to have kept the poorer strata away from church'. Accordingly class-conscious workers gave up attending Sunday services or taking Communion, which could involve mixing with social 'superiors', but they generally continued to marry and baptise their children in church, as this brought them together only with family and neighbours.[1] In the 1890s much the same was happening in Catholic Vienna:

As far as the great majority of artisans is concerned, the religious sense has disappeared. Those among them who do not simply, with careless enlightenment, see this as a sign of progress, attribute the prevailing indifference in religious matters – not without bitterness – to the deeply unchristian behaviour of the dominant and possessing classes towards the proletariat. Because of this the state's promotion of religion among the poor and oppressed looks like a means used by the inwardly unchristian upper classes to protect their class privileges.[2]

This moral critique of the church and of the social uses of religion could as well lead to religious sectarianism as to secularism. But in the late nineteenth century some workers were adopting a dogmatic atheism, in terms of which Darwin and Marx had made God either unbelievable or unnecessary. This, for instance, was the view propagated by the Social Democratic evening classes in Germany. In England this new form of irreligion was grafted onto an older secularist tradition, going back to the 1790s, which had its counter-Bible in Tom Paine's *Age of Reason*. Paine had turned Protestant fundamentalist exegetical techniques to secularist ends by highlighting inconsistencies, absurdities and atrocities in the Christian scriptures. Throughout the nineteenth century he had a good many working-class disciples, and there were even a few places, like the small Lancashire town of Failsworth, where it was possible to grow up in a secularist environment. Here the Secular Society had its roots in a Jacobin Club of the 1790s, and unlike the many short-lived secularist organisations whose whole existence depended on a particular agitation, it had a continuous existence into the 1950s; with its schools, library, band, burial club, it was able to perform many of the wide-ranging social functions of the Nonconformist chapels. In nearby Manchester a secularist family, the Davies of Ancoats, have been described in a fascinating family history. They had been in turn Chartists, secularists, campaigners for birth control, and socialists. Their assumptions were 'cut and dried' and 'bred in': 'They believed, and the experience of three generations lent colour to the belief, that "though there are good bosses and bad bosses, all are concerned in exploiting the working class, and so the proper attitude to the bosses is hostility". They held firmly that "religion is the opium of the people" – propaganda to keep the workers docile and unresisting in the hope of a reward hereafter.' One member of the family, a cotton spinner blacklisted by the employers, was remembered for his enthusiastic reading of Marx and Darwin, a library that also included Plato, Aristotle and Voltaire, and the maxim that 'agnostic is nowt but atheist with a top hat'. 'Pa Holt was what was then called a Determinist, he believed that people were what their heredity and environment made them. He denied "free will" and held that actions followed from a balance of desires.'[3]

However, it may well be that this kind of scientific rationalism contributed less to the mood of working-class irreligion than a feeling of resentment against a God who had done little for the poor. Max Weber, in discussing the importance in most religious systems of the interpretation given to suffering, commented: 'Even as late as 1906, a mere minority among a rather considerable number of proletarians gave as reasons for their disbelief in Christianity conclusions derived from modern theories of natural sciences. The majority, however, referred to the "injustice" of the order of this world – to be sure, essentially because they believed in a revolutionary compensation in this world.' Similarly a survey in Lyon in the 1950s, where church-going Catholics were asked why people whom they knew lacked religious faith or had lost their faith, found that 50 per cent of working-class respondents (but only 15 per cent of those from the well-to-do middle class) mentioned the 'misfortunes and difficulties of life' as a reason. A 'characteristic reply' stated: 'Faced with the misfortunes and difficulties of life, unemployment, housing problems, death, etc., a young man says to his mother: "You can see, mother, how much use taking communion is to you."'[4] Adelheid Popp, a Vienna factory worker, who was a leader of the socialist women's movement in Austria during the 1880s and 1890s, described in her anonymous autobiography, intended as an archetypal story, in which the universal rather than the particular in her experience was stressed, how as a young working girl she often went to church to pray for help, and twice went on pilgrimages, but her prayers had not been answered:

Although there was little in the Social Democratic paper about religion, I was by then free from all religious ideas. It did not happen all at once, but developed slowly. I no longer believed in a God and a better world beyond, but I still sometimes wondered if there was something in it. On the same day that I had tried to prove to the women I worked with that the creation of the world in six days was only a fairy-tale, that there couldn't be an all-powerful God as then there would not be so many people who suffered hard blows from fate, I still put my hands together as I lay in bed and looked up at the picture of Mary. I couldn't help thinking again, 'Well, perhaps after all'. I would never have admitted to anyone that I was troubled by doubts. But I used the revelations in my paper about Siberia and the dreadful things that had happened in the Petersburg prison to prove to my colleagues that there could be no God who influenced the fate of men.[5]

A contemporary of Adelheid Popp's who lived in equally precarious circumstances in the East End of London, described his parents' religious views in somewhat similar terms – though in their case they do not seem to have had any great interest in politics:

Our attitude towards religion was – that somewhere in the skies was a God, the Father of the human race, and the Maker of the World. To certain favoured individuals He was kind, and provided good food and raiment in return for a regular attendance at church. The people in our street, especially our own family had been overlooked by God, and it was foolish to expect deliverance from our troubles by any other source than our own abilities. Thus we felt sure that there was a God, but that He was no friend of ours, that it was of no use to depend on Him for anything, and that it behoved us to sharpen our wits and fight the world for what we could get.[6]

George Acorn, the London cabinet-maker, was eventually to reject his parents' view of the world, and to become an active Nonconformist. Adelheid Popp's story suggests on the other hand, that the discovery of socialism, which she described as 'not only necessary, but world-redeeming', could turn this pessimistic deism into an emphatic denial of God.

II

It is clear, then, that there were many working-class areas where the Christian churches failed to establish themselves effectively in the second half of the nineteenth century, or where their influence seriously declined. This could come about in several different ways. In the first place, working-class immigrants to the cities tended to come from the poorest sections of the rural population, which were sometimes substantially alienated from the church. There were also whole zones of rural Europe where the church had never become very effectively rooted (for example southern Portugal) or had by the mid-nineteenth century largely died out (for example many of the *départements* surrounding Paris). The migrant from such areas brought little in the way of formal religion with him to the city. But even in cities which drew their population from a pious countryside, nineteenth century conditions made it difficult for the migrant to maintain his religious habits: giant parishes made it impossible for the clergy to keep contact with more than a small proportion of their parishioners; many factory workers and small traders were forced to work on Sunday, and so tended to lose the habit of going to church; many poor people were so busy just keeping their heads above water that they had no surplus time, money or energy to spend on the church, or any other institution. Houtart gives these factors a central place in his account of the decline of working-class Catholicism in Brussels: 'the popular classes established themselves on the margins of the ecclesiastical organisation of the time, which did not correspond to their needs. . . . The documents seem to indicate that at the time of their arrival in the town they still practised regularly. But the hardness of life, uprooting, depersonalisation, the lack of church buildings and priests, meant that they gradually abandoned religious practice'.[7] There were also cities where the church did have strong working-class support in the first half of the nineteenth century, but subsequently lost it. The case of Marseille was discussed in an earlier chapter. There was a similar story in Barmen. Here the 'old Wuppertal traditions' survived longest among domestic textile workers belonging to local families; but these traditions became an increasingly marginal feature of the city's working-class life from the 1860s and 1870s, with large scale immigration from other parts of Germany, the rise of factory industry, increasing class antagonism, the propaganda of the socialists, and the growing feeling that the church was an ally of the capitalists. Wolfgang Köllmann, the historian of Barmen, writes that in the 1870s and 1880s the spiritual vacuum in the lives of workers tended to be filled by a socialism that took the form of a 'substitute religion with salvationist tendencies'.[8]

Yet Köllmann denies that the result was a general 'dechristianisation' of the city's workers, and there are indeed several respects in which this widely current concept needs to be modified. In the first place, militant irreligion was much more common among men than among women. In the industrial cities of late nineteenth-century Europe there were probably a great many families in which, while the husband was loudly proclaiming his contempt for church and religion, the wife was quietly bringing up the children in the ancestral faith. Even in 1956, when 36 per cent of working-class men questioned in a French poll said they were without religion or were religiously indifferent, only 19 per cent of working-class women said so; and while 16 per cent of working-class men said they were 'practising' a religion, 42 per cent of working-class women said they were.[9] Further points, each of which will be discussed in turn, are that many of those who rejected the church on political or social grounds continued to regard themselves as Christians; that there were some working-class communities in which the church continued to flourish throughout the nineteenth century, and well into the twentieth; and that the religious beliefs and allegiances of many working-class people were too complex and ambivalent to be easily categorised either as 'Christian' or 'non-Christian'.

The relationship between political radicalism and Christianity was especially complex in Britain. As a counter-type to the secularist Davies family one could quote the family tradition of Wesley Perrins, a former Black Country nailer who was a Labour M.P. from 1945 to 1950.[10] Perrins' grandfather was remembered for strongarm action against blacklegs, and for the fact that the men in his workshop would club together to buy a *Reynolds News*, which he, as the only one who was literate, would read to them. His father and sisters had long records of sackings for political and trade union activities. In the Perrins family these seem to have gone hand in hand with Methodism, and Wesley Perrins took the view that 'the Labour movement in this part of the country was, in its origins, very largely a Christian crusade. It was a practical application of Christian faith, an agitation to uplift the poor, to improve working conditions that were often unbelievably bad.' Perrins' father, a Methodist Sunday School superintendent, had been a Liberal, but in 1918 transferred to Labour, and was one of the first Labour councillors in Stourbridge. Although in Perrins' account the switch appears natural and painless, it is clear from other accounts of this period that the contest between Liberal and Labour was often bitter, and the role of the Nonconformist churches in the conflict often caused much resentment on the Labour side. In the 1892 election the support of the Nonconformist ministers for the Liberal candidate in Bradford led many of the supporters of the Labour candidate to form their own Labour church – one of about a hundred set up in the 1890s by those who felt that 'the Christian Churches have been . . . captured by the capitalist' and that 'the employed should have their own Church, their own service which shall be to them a Sunday home'.[11] Robert Moore's study of a group of Durham mining villages shows how the Methodists, who controlled the union lodges and a variety of other local institutions at the end of the nineteenth century, used their power in the interests of political Liberalism and industrial conciliation. When the challenge came in the early twentieth century from a more class-conscious younger generation, adhering to the Independent Labour Party, the leaders of the revolt were mostly Methodists too, but they occupied a more marginal position in their chapels, and they faced opposition from the chapel leadership. They also were often unorthodox in their theology. It was not easy, therefore, to reconcile their socialist politics with continuing membership of their church, and many of them left, or ceased to take an active part in chapel life. But they often continued to stress the 'spiritual' objectives of socialism, and there were many who, like Keir Hardie, saw the labour movement as the true exponents of a Christianity that the churches had largely abandoned.

While in Britain no clear-cut division between church and labour movement existed, even in countries where the Left was explicitly anti-church, and the church was officially anti-socialist, there was not necessarily any simple equation between the rise of socialism and the decline of Christianity. A study of Saxony in 1902 referred to the walls where the pictures of the socialist leader, August Bebel, hung beside Luther and King Albert of Saxony, and the author commented: 'In the soul of the people, it looks just like it does on the wall: it brings together harmlessly the things that are most opposed.' Or as an American student of French working-class politics in the 1940s and 1950s remarked: 'Unlike the popular American analyses wherein people are either one thing or the other (one is either Communist *or* Catholic) it seems likely that many workers are trying to be both – to maintain some commitment to *both* faiths.' He quoted various French communities where Communist voting was high and church attendance by men low, but 'everyone is confirmed, baptised, married and buried by the Church' and 'the wives of local Communists go to Mass almost as faithfully as those of the local bourgeoisie'.[12] The rise of socialism certainly weakened the influence of the clergy, and perhaps in the longer term facilitated the spread of religious indifference. But in the shorter term it did not necessarily mean any widespread atheism.

In Britain, in fact, throughout this period, the majority of working-class people were neither deeply committed church members, nor did they have strong radical or anti-religious convictions. Their religious ideas tended to be fluid, eclectic, and, from the point of view of churchman or militant unbeliever, incoherent. For instance, Richard Hoggart, in recalling the Leeds of his childhood in the 1930s, included a section on 'primary religion'. This consisted of: belief in the purposiveness of life – 'we're here for a purpose'; belief in an after-life, bringing release and relief; the great importance attached to funerals; the belief that religion is mainly ethics, and that 'all this dogma' is no help – Christian ethics are good but 'religious mania' must be avoided; ritual is no use; a generally pragmatic attitude – religious principles are admirable, but you can't stick to them too literally in everyday life. In other sections he noted the strong belief in luck: 'The world of experience is mapped at every point, particularly closely at the great nodes, into two colours, into those things which "mean good luck" and those which "mean bad luck"'. The core of working-class life he saw as 'a sense of the personal, the concrete, the local': the sense of neighbourhood is strong, and the family is the great sacred institution; a strong group sense is manifested in suspicion of change and insensitivity towards the deviant; on the other hand, there is suspicion towards and continual debunking of 'them'. 'Politics', 'social philosophy' and 'metaphysics' attract little interest. The main thing is to keep cheerful and try to enjoy life – as trouble will come anyway.[13]

Many similar ideas were current in later nineteenth-century London, where we have the evidence of such classic contemporary accounts as Charles Booth's *Life and Labour*. Here most working-class parents had their children christened and sent them to Sunday School, and they themselves might belong to a church social club. But formal church attendance was largely limited to certain solemn moments in life, when there was no substitute for the dignity and sanctity provided by the church – in the annual cycle only Watch Night (rather than any specifically Christian festival) really came into this category, though in more recent times Remembrance Sunday would qualify. Churching, christening, marriage in church, were generally practised, but these were less important occasions in working-class life than funerals. It was then that church and clergyman were most necessary to assert the sacredness of a human life, to provide some comfort to those often suddenly and tragically bereaved, to offer some hope of a happier world beyond.

Judgement had no place in the popular conception of the after-life. As the saying was 'We have our hell here' and eternity could be conceived of only in terms of sleep or of rest and relief. Indeed the whole scheme of sin, atonement, grace, as understood by evangelicals and Catholics, had little place in the religion of most working-class people. From this point of view, what evangelicals call 'the Gospel' was merely 'dogma', and as such irrelevant to the substance of Christianity, which was ethics, or to the availability of supernatural aid in times of crisis. Nor did the idea of a set-apart community of believers appeal to most working-class people: it smacked of a desire to put on airs, or to curry favour with social superiors. Christianity was seen essentially as decent behaviour, and Jesus as a supreme moral teacher. Going to church did not help, as the super-pious were usually hypocrites; doctrines of sin and grace were no use, as decent living was within everyone's capabilities, and more than that could not be hoped for.

Various aspects of their social situation and experience tended to limit the contact of working-class people with organised religious bodies. The powerful sense of community solidarity led to a suspicion of anyone who was conspicuously different. The general lack of interest in dogma, theory, abstraction, as things remote from the everyday practice of life, was reflected in an indifference to theology. The recognition that life is hard, and rogues abound, tended to produce scepticism, fatalism, and an exaggerated distrust of idealists and the apparently virtuous. The experience of subordination, of being victim rather than agent, led to cynicism about the possibility of significant change, or the value of action, except *ad hoc* and on a very local scale. The puritanism of many religious groups was also repudiated: the pleasures life brings may be few, but they should be enjoyed – 'A little of what you fancy does you good'.[14]

III

Nonetheless, there were areas of nineteenth-century Britain where working class church attendance was still quite high in the later nineteenth century. It was 15–20 per cent in the East End of London or in the poorer districts of Birmingham (and quite a high proportion of these congregations would be made up of shopkeepers and small employers); but it was around 40 per cent in working-class areas of Bristol, where Nonconformists predominated, and in the Catholic wards of Liverpool. The 1851 religious census had shown that there were a number of industrial districts where probably a majority of the population attended church or chapel, including south Wales, some of the mining and nailing communities of the Black Country, and some of the weaving districts of north-east Lancashire. These were areas of villages and small towns, with few middle-class inhabitants, where organised religion was heavily Nonconformist.

In most parts of Britain, church involvement has declined a good deal since the later nineteenth century. But in a number of the industrial regions of western Europe the Catholic church continued to have an active working-class following in to the 1950s and 1960s. These were mostly places where Catholics were a disadvantaged minority (Northern Ireland, the Rhineland, the Netherlands), or where Catholicism had become closely bound up with the identity of a disadvantaged language community (the Basques in Spain, the Flemish-speakers in Belgium and France). In such circumstances shared adversity has tended to bring Catholic workers and the relatively small Catholic middle class together, and to weaken the impact of the internal social antagonisms that in most other situations have tended to split the Catholic community on class lines. The ground has thus been very favourable for the establishment of a highly organised Catholic sub-culture, providing for most of the needs of its members, and isolating them from contacts with outsiders. One such area would be the Belgian Limburg, since 1901 a centre of mining, and of metal and chemical industries, where in the early 1950s some 80 per cent of the population were practising Catholics. Factors accounting for the church's continuing strength include the area's isolation, and the system of Catholic trade unions and workers' associations. In the latter respect, the relatively late industrialisation may have been an advantage to the church, as in 1920 the Belgian socialists were far ahead of the Catholics in organising the workers; but in the 1920s and 1930s the Catholics narrowed the gap, and by 1963 the majority of unionised workers, both manual and white-collar, belonged to Catholic unions. Another area where a strong Catholic trade union movement developed in the 1920s and 1930s was the textile district of northern France, especially the cities of Roubaix, Tourcoing and Armentières – though here it had to compete with an anti-clerical socialism that was already well established. This was one of the few industrial areas of France where the network of parishes kept pace with the growth of population in the later nineteenth and early twentieth centuries; it also seems to have produced quite a large number of 'democratic priests', who avoided the over-close ties with the local bourgeoisie that compromised the church in many parts of France. Equally important, probably, was the strong appeal of the church to the large number of Belgian immigrants (a majority of the population in late nineteenth-century Roubaix), who were treated with contempt by many of their French neighbours.

The rest of this chapter will look at two religions of the working class which won a large following in the nineteenth century, though in one instance the early twentieth century brought a marked decline: south-Wales Nonconformity, and the Catholicism of the Irish immigrant ghettos in England and Scotland.

The assumption that industrialisation in itself led to a weakening of organised religion is called in question by the example of south Wales. In the later eighteenth and early nineteenth centuries the almost empty mountain valleys of north-east Glamorgan and north Monmouthshire were filled with iron-works and with a new population of factory-workers drawn from all over Wales and western England. A mass of small Nonconformist chapels were set up by these immigrants and, especially in Welsh-speaking communities, they won the support of a very large section of the population. The 1851 religious census showed that in Merthyr Tydfil, the leading iron-town, church attendance was higher than in any other large town of England and Wales, excepting only Colchester. While perhaps a third of the working-class population of this area never attended church and chapel, and found the focus of its free hours in the pubs and benefit societies, there was a large hard-core of active church-members, many of whom were lay preachers or Sunday School teachers, and another large group of so-called 'hearers' who regularly attended chapel, without ever becoming members. As the owners and managers of the iron-works were nearly all English, and in religious terms Anglican, the Nonconformist population was heavily working-class, the more so since the prevalence of company shops inhibited the growth of a shop-keeping lower-middle class. In these proletarian communities the most influential individuals were Nonconformist preachers, and the chapels were uniquely important cultural and educational, as well as religious centres.

While the chapels still had a powerful influence in the early twentieth century, the basis for their decline was laid in the years after 1860 when a largely Welsh-owned and managed coal industry replaced iron as the basis of the region's economy. The result of this was an increasing divide within the chapels between a middle-class élite, well represented in the 'big pew', and the working-class people sitting behind. It is significant that the first big drop in chapel adherence came in 1898, for that was the year of a big strike which signalled the start of a period of intense conflict in the mines. In the next few years socialists began to replace the old Liberal leadership in the miners' unions, and the Independent Labour Party established a large following, while the chapels remained closely tied to the Liberal Party. Although the revival of 1904–5 brought a temporary return to the chapels, its influence was short-lived. While the decline in the influence of the mainly Welsh-speaking chapels was in part an aspect of the general decline of Welsh culture under the impact of English immigration, the decisive factor seems to have been class conflict, the identification of the chapels with one side of an increasingly polarised community, and the rival attractions of a socialism which was generally condemned by a Nonconformity preoccupied with individual salvation and the battle against the established church.

A second example of a working-class community in which the church had a central role for a long period is that of the Irish diaspora formed in Britain from the 1790s, and more especially from the potato famine of the 1840s.

Where not alienated from the working class by alliance with the political Right and social élites, the Catholic church has sometimes shown an unusual degree of success in retaining the loyalty of impoverished populations. Even in the 1960s, Catholic practice in Britain, though low by Irish standards, was far above the national average: in 1961, weekly attendance at mass was estimated as 41 per cent of Catholics aged seven and over in England and Wales.[15] During the second half of the nineteenth century strong Catholic parishes were formed in the Irish ghettos of London, Liverpool, Glasgow, and indeed most other large towns; and the parish church, with its great network of organisations for each class of Catholic became a focal point of immigrant life. The exclusion, and sometimes violence suffered by the Irish strengthened the sense of group identity of which their Catholicism was partly an expression: in Cardiff, for instance, in 1848, the murder of a Welshman by an Irish navvy had provoked a Welsh mob to attack houses in the Irish district, and smash all the windows of the church, and the outcry caused by the restoration of the Catholic hierarchy in 1850 led the Catholic authorities to place Irish guards on London churches. The concentration of the Irish in certain districts and occupations further strengthened this group identity and facilitated the church's system of controls, especially after a comprehensive network of Catholic schools had been established.

There were indeed a good many immigrant Catholics who were very irregular in the practice of their faith, and some who lost touch with the church entirely. These were drawn especially from the poorest sections of the Irish population, many of whom found their energies fully absorbed in the struggle for survival, regarded the church (and all other movements or institutions) with apathy or embitterment, or found all their solace in the public house. There were also many poor Irish who found their escape-route in crime or prostitution. Militant Irish nationalism or more general radical and trade union activity offered other alternatives which sometimes brought their adherents into conflict with a conservative church. But the church was still the central institution of the Irish community, entering in one way or another into the lives of many who seldom went to mass. One reason for this was the continuity of habits and assumptions brought over from Ireland. Though the church was often unable to keep pace with Irish immigration and many lapsed from Catholic practice for want of churches and priests, subsequent efforts to form parishes in these areas usually met with a widespread response: in significant contrast to the great programme of Anglican church-building in previously neglected city parishes from about the 1840s on, which often resulted in a lot of large half-empty churches. Another advantage possessed by the Catholic church in Britain as against its counterparts in France and elsewhere was the absence of any compromising association with the state, though this of course carried the corresponding disadvantage that the priests had to be constantly on the lookout for contributions from their flock. Moreover, priestly despotism, the slow pace of upward mobility within the Catholic population, and the availability of large numbers of small contributors inhibited the development of the dominating oligarchy found in many Nonconformist chapels. There had in fact been signs of such tendencies in the early nineteenth century. In one of many such comments, Gentili, the famous Italian missionary to England, reported from Chelsea in 1846 that 'The parish contains a vast number of poor who never come to Mass, because they have to pay to enter any part of the church, except for a small area reserved to them'. Many of the new urban churches established in the later eighteenth and early nineteenth century were managed by lay trustees drawn from the substantial middle class; these being elected by an élite of 'bench-holders' who occupied the front seats in the church, while the poor sat at the back or in the gallery.[16] From about the 1840s, when lay power was already a lost cause, the symbols of privilege were under attack from a new generation of clergy, primarily conscious of their mission to the Irish, willing to contact them by visiting door to door or preaching in the street, to attract them by colourful services and sensational sermons of a type alien to English Catholic tradition, and to pull down the galleries and abolish the door money that might frighten them away. The priests were the lynch-pins of the system. The strength of the working-class Catholic parish from about the 1840s until the 1960s depended on clerical initiative, and the willingness of Irish immigrants and their descendants to respond to these initiatives. Its double vulnerability lay, on the one hand, in the fact that these priests were insufficient in numbers and often unequal to their task, and, on the other, in the strong undercurrent of resentment that was provoked by the authoritarianism intrinsic to the priest's role. It was the priests who wielded the force of community pressure against those who wanted to marry Protestants, who accepted Protestant charity or sent their children to Protestant schools; the priest who denounced sinners from the pulpit, who squeezed from his impoverished parishioners the funds needed to build their church and school, support their priests, teachers, and parochial charities, who induced them to sign petitions and told them how to vote; who harried the mass-missers.

Between priest and people there was, as Sheridan Gilley writes in his fine study of the London Irish, 'a semi-paternal relationship compounded of love and fear'.[17] This priestly discipline was effective because of the widespread support enjoyed by the clergy within the Irish community, enhanced both by their devotion to their people, and by the superstitious regard that led so many negligent Catholics to send for the priest in illness, whether from the fear of hell or from the belief that the priest was 'endowed with the power of healing diseases'.[18] The tie was further strengthened in the second half of the nineteenth century by an Ultramontane piety, repellent to Protestants (and to many English Catholics), but attractive to many poor immigrants: statues of Mary began to fill the once bare churches, while spectacular missions mixed hell-fire oratory with such special attractions as indulgences for kissing a ten-foot-high cross on a high brick platform 'with the scourges hanging from the arms, the sacred monogram nailed above the red thorn crown, and the lance and sponge affixed to the pole'.[19]

The system worked fairly well as long as priestly despotism was both practicable and acceptable. It fell into decline in the 1920s as rehousing schemes broke up the old Irish ghettos, and more especially in the 1960s and 1970s. By then the decline of clerical recruitment made the old system increasingly unpracticable and Vatican II called in question most of the assumptions that had dominated the British Catholicism of the last century and a half. Meanwhile a more educated Catholic community was rebelling against large areas of the church's teaching and practice, and in 1968 the Pope's condemnation of contraceptives focussed lay discontent as no single issue had ever done before.

The Irish Catholics in Britain suffered to the full the characteristic living and working conditions of nineteenth-century urban proletarians, and the characteristic deficiencies of church machinery in nineteenth-century cities. But their experience suggests that while factors of this sort certainly put their Catholicism under strain, they do not necessarily lead to, and are insufficient to explain the conscious alienation from the church or from religion that was developing in many working class communities at that time. Alienation of this kind was primarily a product of class relationships.

8 Fragmentation

I

In the 1950s there was a spate of sociological studies of parishes or of religious attitudes, many of them written by clergymen. The German sociologist, Thomas Luckmann, summarised their conclusions by suggesting that 'church-oriented religion has become a marginal phenomenon in modern society', and that the church's social base had shrunk to 'peripheral' groups, such as peasants, the lower middle class and the old. He went on to argue that a sociology of religion that was relevant to modern conditions would largely ignore the church. This judgement was premature.[1] If Luckmann's definition of the church's social base was reasonably applicable to the Protestant areas of Germany (where most of his evidence came from), it was quite inadequate to describe the situation in countries like France and Spain, where the most powerful sections of the urban population were those closest to the Catholic church. There were also many respects in which the church wielded considerable social power in itself. In the majority of west-European countries it had an important part in the educational system, and in some it maintained an extensive network of charitable institutions. Above all, the period from about 1945–65 was a golden age for the 'Christian Democratic' parties in many parts of Europe. In old strongholds of confessionalism, like the Low Countries, religious parties continued to have a decisive role in the political system; and in the immediate aftermath of war, religion seemed a good rallying point for new parties in France and Germany which were hoping to establish themselves around the centre of the political spectrum, with a cross-class appeal. In the 1960s, religion was still the best indicator of how a person would vote in France, and probably in Belgium and the Netherlands.[2]

In Britain and Scandinavia the political influence and institutional strength of the churches was a good deal less, and Luckmann's references to the 'marginality' of 'church-oriented religion' were more plausible. He would presumably have had the agreement of Herbert Tingsten, a prominent Swedish political scientist, who wrote in a newspaper article of 1949 that most Swedish Christians were:

Christians-in-name-only (*namnkristna*), indeed, the phrase Christians-in-name-only seems almost too strong even when used to designate total indifference bounded by approval of tradition and convention. They say they believe in God, yet do not accept the doctrines that distinguish Christianity. They want to keep education in Christianity, yet do not go to church. Baptism, confirmation, marriage, and burial – these are the contacts these people have, not with religion (for there is no reason to have such contact!) but only with the church. The holy sacraments provide a setting for festive occasions. A necessity for this state of affairs is that they do not listen, do not understand, or at least do not pay any attention to what is said. They enquire as little into the meaning of these things as they ponder electricity on a journey by tram. This we all know, and this we all say – but convention is so well established that it is considered a trifle unbecoming to say so publicly.[3]

No doubt the same comments could have been made in Denmark, where in the mid 1960s 95 per cent of the population belonged to the Lutheran church, and where weekly church attendance varied between 2 per cent in the capital and 4 per cent in the most devout rural region. Yet it may well be that Tingsten's cut and dried categories miss most of the complexities and ambiguities in the relationship between the mass of 'Christians-in-name-only' and their churches. There may be greater value in the more tentative comment of a Danish sociologist who suggested on the basis of his inquiry into attitudes to the rites of passage in Copenhagen 'that the Danish people is a religious people, and that the Dane stands in need of a religious institution. The State Church cannot meet these religious wants, but it is the only institution we have – at least the only big and competitive institution at hand.'[4]

The same comment would probably have been applicable to Britain, though the minority of active church members was bigger (especially in Wales and Scotland), and the multiplicity of denominations meant that no single church held such a dominant position as the Lutheran state churches. Even so, the parish system still gave the Church of England and the Church of Scotland a uniquely comprehensive coverage of the population, and if the churches often had a very superficial influence, nothing had very effectively taken their place. As one example, a study of poverty in Nottingham could be cited, which showed that about 20 per cent of those interviewed were church members. This figure might be taken as a reflection of the degree of secularisation in the district, but instead the authors suggested that: 'the striking thing is that with all the labour of secular agitation that remains to be done in St. Ann's, the churches, particularly the little churches, are at the top of the organisational league'.[5] A slightly different point is illustrated by a series of interviews with elderly inhabitants of Poplar in London's dockland, an area where church attendance is probably as low as anywhere in England, and was already low when the respondents were born around the beginning of this century. A book based on these interviews included a chapter on 'Religion and the Community', which was mainly about notable clergymen (mostly Anglo-Catholic or Methodist) who had worked in the area, and which suggested that 'in Poplar, the priest tends to be drawn into the community feeling'. Certainly clergymen continually cropped up in the interviews and it is clear that many of them made a big impact as personalities, and that whether through Sunday Schools or church day schools, church social clubs, visiting, or political activities, they established themselves as familiar, and sometimes popular, figures in an ostensibly non-church-going community. In fact some of the comments of those who were most critical of the clergy in general are suggestive of a popular ideal of the good vicar which many people would respond to enthusiastically when they met it. One man, after his wife had made approving comments about various local clergymen, compared them unfavourably with St. John Groser, the famous Anglo-Catholic and left-wing socialist vicar of Christ Church, Stepney:

Well they were alright outside. But when they went inside they had their wine and a cigar. I'm not so sure. Not like John. He lived like a Labour man – 'All I want is two potatoes and a small piece of beef.' He lived a Christian life. He was one of the few who came away from the usual run of vicars and said we are with the people and should live like the people . . .

Comments like this suggest not the blank indifference described by Tingsten, but a lively ideal of Christian living, and the possibility of real disappointment when it is not realised. A similar comment was that of a former chairman of the Poplar Labour Party who had been a member of All Hallows church at the time of the dock strike in 1912: 'They had some very enthusiastic parsons up there – they preached the Gospel as to my mind it should be preached . . . they were great people – different to-day, much different.'[6] Perhaps because of this ideal, the church, however peripheral to most people's lives for most of the time, remained an important resource in times of trouble and a potential source of local leadership.

II

Yet by the late 1960s it already seemed that the information painstakingly collected by the 'religious sociologists' of the previous decade was hopelessly out of date. From about 1967 the Churches were in a state of crisis in most parts of western Europe. There was a general decline in church attendance; many churches lost members; large numbers of priests were resigning, and there were few newcomers to take their places; in some countries there was quite a big drop in the proportion of couples going through a religious marriage ceremony or baptising their children; the confessional parties were all losing votes. Even in Britain, where the churches were already relatively weak, the years 1965–70 saw a larger percentage decline in membership than any previous period this century; in the many Catholic countries where church influence was still strong in the 1940s and 1950s, at least in middle-class and peasant areas, the decline in the religious indices in the later 1960s and early 1970s was more spectacular, and the effects of these years far more traumatic. The following section will look at three very different examples of societies where the church faced a crisis in the 1960s: East Germany, the Netherlands and Spain.

The only west-European government to pursue a deliberately anti-religious policy in the period since 1945 has been the Socialist Unity regime which has held power in the German Democratic Republic since the state's foundation in 1949. The Socialist Unity Party was the result of the forced amalgamation of the often reluctant Social Democrats with the Communists in the Soviet occupation zone. In power it has been inspired by the militant irreligion of the Communists, rather than the more eclectic religious traditions of the Social Democrats, who were mainly hostile to the church, but had included a number of 'religious socialists' among their supporters in the Weimar period. While the attack on religion has taken less violent forms than in, for instance, the Soviet Union, and the churches have continued to enjoy more rights than in some of the neighbouring Communist-ruled countries, the early 1950s saw the imprisonment of a number of clergymen and lay activists, and since then the government has continued to encourage the propagation of atheism, and to discourage continued membership of the churches. The chief means of doing this have been the Marxist-atheist slant of the education provided in the schools and in the state youth movements, discrimination against children of church-goers in the schools, and the exclusion of those who retain their links with the churches from most positions of power and influence. These policies seem to have had a fair amount of success so far, as the proportion of the population of East Germany declared to be 'without religion' at censuses increased from 8 per cent in 1946, to 31 per cent in 1964, and about 40 per cent in 1974. It seems that the Protestant churches and the small Catholic church have been about equally hit by these defections. In the same period the number of baptisms and of religious marriages and funerals has also fallen considerably, the number of Protestants attending church has dropped, and the shortage of funds and personnel has meant that rural parishes often have no pastors, and new towns have no church buildings. One recent study suggested that a quarter of the decline in church adherence could be explained by flight to the West (which was very considerable in the 1950s, and may have included a disproportionate number of church members), and that most of the rest was a result of secularisation associated with industrialisation, 'with only a small part attributable to atheist propaganda'.[7] It seems unlikely that this explanation is sufficient, since there has been no comparable movement out of the churches in the equally industrialised (and secularised) West Germany, where 96 per cent of the population claimed a religious affiliation at the 1961 census.

In fact, if regular church attendance were the test, the difference between East and West Germany would probably be much slighter. But the effect of state policy has been to reveal the fragility of the 'people's church' (*Volkskirche*), to use the phrase current in Germany and Scandinavia, with its overwhelmingly high nominal membership, paying its church taxes, and coming to church for the rites of passage, its highly educated and respectable clergy, its conservative and patriotic traditions, close ties with the state, and low active membership. In East Germany the atheist state has shown that fairly rapid inroads into this impressive nominal membership can be made by presenting disincentives to continued participation in the church's rituals, and sometimes by introducing alternatives, notably the Youth Dedication Ceremony (*Jugendweihe*), which has to quite a large extent replaced Confirmation, though some adolescents go through both.

If the East German authorities have so far been fairly successful in their short-term aim of reducing the influence of the churches, it does not necessarily follow that they have succeeded in raising a generation of convinced atheists. Certainly the numerous Soviet investigations in this field suggest that while a majority of those questioned will always claim to be atheists, just as a majority of those questioned in most western surveys will claim to believe in God, the number of well-informed and consistent atheists is small, and besides nominal atheists who maintain some sort of Christian tradition (for instance, having icons in their house), there are a lot of others who adhere to magical beliefs of one sort or another.[8] Nor does the rapid drop in the churches' nominal membership necessarily mean a decline in the vigour of the more active membership – already small in most parts of northern Germany long before 1945. The evidence on the latter point is at present unclear – and certainly depends very much on subjective impressions. For instance a committee appointed by the British Council of Churches which investigated religious conditions in Communist-ruled countries in the early 1970s, was eulogistic of the Protestant churches in East Germany (though rather critical of the Catholics), praising the political independence of the Protestant church leadership, the liveliness of the student parishes, the high academic standards in the theological faculties, and the usefulness of the church's social work. A report by a West German political scientist at about the same time presented the Protestant church membership as demoralised, and its leaders as vacillating (but praised the Catholics). Meanwhile a pastor who surveyed the situation at parish level was pessimistic and hopeful in about equal measures, stressing on the one hand the preponderance in many congregations of old people, often having little interest in or sympathy with either contemporary East German society or modern theological ideas; and on the other hand the lively experimentation in areas like the universities and the new towns, where church membership was small, but highly active and responsible.[9] It would seem that, as in most other Communist-ruled countries, some of the support for the church is motivated by rejection of the political system and a consequent adoption of what is the only alternative ideology. The official position of the church leadership is rather different: a 'critical solidarity', which takes the form of acceptance of the socialist objectives of the regime, but a willingness to criticise the means chosen for their realisation. It is not clear at present how much support this position has among the rank and file of church members, or how much influence it has on the general population, though it is interesting to note that Rudolf Bahro, the dissident East German Communist who was recently forced to emigrate to West Germany, has appealed for the common action by Marxists and Christians in a spirit of mutual learning which is implicitly being demanded by the East German Protestant church, while being effectively rejected by the government.[10]

While the Protestant areas of northern Germany – homeland, appropriately enough, both of Nietzsche, and of Bonhöffer, the most famous interpreter of Christianity in the context of a godless world – have long been among the most secularised in the Christian world, the Catholic areas of the Netherlands stood at almost the opposite extreme in the second half of the nineteenth century and the first half of the twentieth. During this period the Dutch Catholics became one of the most highly organised sections of the church, and in spite of fairly high levels of urbanisation and industrialisation, and the proximity of large communities of Protestants and of unbelievers, they remained among the most devout. Yet they too experienced dramatic changes in the 1960s. The chief reason for this was the catalytic effect of the Second Vatican Council (1962–5) in speeding up the process by which the 'pillarisation' of Dutch society broke down, and Catholics were accordingly released from their social isolation, and subjected to the pressures of a pluralist society. The Catholic ghetto had been a practical means of making Catholicism a force in a Protestant-dominated society, and protecting the faith and identity of Catholics from aggressive Protestantism or socialism. It was no longer so relevant in the 1950s and 1960s, when a relatively prosperous and educated Catholic community had for many years enjoyed a pivotal position in the Dutch political system, and both socialists and Dutch Reformed had long lost any taste for anti-Catholic crusades.

The Second Vatican Council was called by Pope John XXIII as a means of reviewing the Catholic church's doctrine, worship and social practice, and adapting them to contemporary religious conditions and ways of thought. In the Netherlands there were signs of growing lay discontent in the 1950s. But during the preparations for Vatican II the Dutch bishops effectively seized the leadership of the nascent reform movement by advocating ideas that were to become a new orthodoxy during the Council, and which would have an explosive effect when put into practice in their own country: pluriformity and decentralisation in the church, lay responsibility, the rights of conscience, co-operation with other churches, and abandonment of Roman Catholicism's exclusive claims. The Dutch bishops and theologians came to be recognised as the avant-garde of the church, and in the early stages of the Council, they, together with some of their colleagues from neighbouring countries, were in fierce conflict with Vatican officials who wanted to keep change to a minimum. The whole Dutch church seemed to be carried along by a wave of enthusiasm for reform: it was estimated that 20 per cent of the whole Catholic population took part in the diocesan discussion groups where priests and laypeople met to discuss the issues that were being decided at Rome.

When the bishops tried to put these decisions into practice, it soon became clear that this unity was threatened from two directions. On the one side were those, in the student parishes for instance, who wanted a much more thorough-going democratisation of the church: their concern for individual conscience and their objection to the set-apart position of the clergy was focussed especially on the right of priests to marry, and in the late 1960s and early 1970s a number of Dutch priests defied the authority of their bishops by continuing to preach and administer the sacraments to their parishioners after marrying. The radical wing of the church also felt that the Catholic authorities were much too cautious in their approach to questions of peace and social injustice, and they wanted the church to be firmly identified with the political left. On the other hand, from 1964 on, conservative Catholics were organising to oppose their bishops, claiming that some were betraying Catholic orthodoxy, while others had feebly abandoned their responsibilities for leadership and discipline. Some of the conservatives had contacts with Rome, and from 1968 the Vatican intervened on several occasions to curb the progress of reform in the Netherlands. Meanwhile the unaccustomed climate of general criticism was proving a powerful solvent of the unity and isolation that had been the basis of the immense institutional strength of Dutch Catholicism. Catholics were beginning to escape from the ghetto. From 1963 to 1967 votes for the Catholic People's Party fell by a quarter; there was a relatively small increase in the proportion of confessionally mixed marriages during the 1960s, but a complete change of attitudes – by 1970 only 21 per cent of Catholics were opposed to these in principle; weekly church attendance, which had been dropping in the larger cities in the 1950s, fell nationally from 64 per cent of Catholics in 1966 to 35 per cent in 1974; resignations from the priesthood increased sharply in the late 1960s; and by this time contraception, a major source of dissension within the church elsewhere, seems to have become generally practised by Catholic laypeople, and regarded as a matter of private conscience by their bishops and parish priests. For the time being relatively few Catholics actually abandoned their faith, and by comparison with their co-religionists in neighbouring countries they remained a strongly church-oriented group. But it was clear that in the future their faith would be of a very different kind: more independent, more personal, and much more vulnerable to the ideas and mores of the surrounding world, and to the attractions of the greater freedom apparently enjoyed by their non-Catholic compatriots.

In Spain too the 1960s and early 1970s were a time of crisis for the Catholic church. The church had formed close links with Franco during and after the civil war, and in the 1940s going to mass became an expression of respectability and political orthodoxy. It may well be that the horrors of the 1930s also contributed to the Catholic revival, persuading many that the Catholic faith provided an inspiration for the rebuilding of the devastated nation, and a basis for the reconciliation of former enemies. In the 1940s large numbers of new priests came forward to take the place of those killed in the war, and many new churches were built. However, the revival was largely limited to those sections of the population that were loyal to the regime. There remained huge differentials between the levels of religious practice in different social groups and in different regions. In the 1960s ecclesiastical, political and economic changes would all contribute to a very rapid change in the character of the Spanish church, and a weakening of its social base.

Here too Vatican II had both a revitalising and a disruptive effect, filling many laypeople and parish priests with hopes for the reform of church and society that the bishops would reject, and eventually leading many of them to leave the church, and in some cases to switch their hopes to the Marxist cause. From about 1967 there was a big movement of resignations from the priesthood, and about the same time there seemed to be a general movement away from the church. By 1973 a Catholic sociologist could refer to a religiosity that was 'sinking with incredible speed, while its fundamental support throughout its history, monolithic orthodoxy and the rejection of pluralism, has been swallowed up by the new cultural currents now in vigorous operation'.[11] Of these, one was the impact of the new conceptions of the Catholic faith associated with Vatican II. Equally important was general discontent with the Franco regime, and consequent rejection of a church which had been among Franco's closest allies – although by the late 1960s, the leaders of the church were distancing themselves from the aged dictator, and at the local level many priests were involved in defence of workers' rights or in regionalist movements. Also, more complex economic changes were weakening the position of the churches in the 1960s. As in other parts of Europe, the 1950s and 1960s saw the decline of peasant agriculture, migration to the city, industrial development, growth of the leisure industry and of tourism, and unprecedented prosperity – with the difference that in Spain these changes were taking place more rapidly and had much more novelty. The fishing and agricultural communities of the Costa Brava, transformed by the development of a huge tourist industry, offer one microcosm of the changes in Spain: areas previously well insulated from contact with the mores of the outside world were suddenly faced with completely different rhythms of work, a potentially very big increase in their standard of living, and new models of behaviour, that seem to have been reflected most clearly in the changing sexual mores of the young.[12] In this situation the church could easily be discredited by its associations with the era of austerity, political repression, and antiquated morality, and the various forms of radicalised Catholicism that had survived the Council period had a narrower appeal than the pursuit of material improvement.

III

These examples illustrate the continuing influence of specific historical inheritances on contemporary religious patterns. But the fragmentation of religious life in the 1960s had its origins in longer-term social changes, including the weakening of communal ties, and the widespread emergence of fully pluralist societies.

By the 1960s a pluralist religious and political order had become more or less firmly established in all parts of western Europe except for the authoritarian states of East Germany, Spain and Portugal, and in Northern Ireland, where the dominant community had been able to maintain the apparatus of religious privilege and discrimination, and sectarian consciousness was still a lively reality. Elsewhere the totalitarian hopes of Protestants and Catholics, liberals and socialists had been largely abandoned, and the political-religious communities that had confronted one another in a spirit of total antagonism around the turn of the century had come to recognise the reality of their existence side by side, and the inevitability of compromise and sometimes co-operation between them. Most socialist and communist parties had given up the attack on religion as counter-productive, and under Pope John XXIII the Catholic church became officially committed to the principle of co-operation with non-Christians in the cause of social justice. The great education wars of earlier years had usually ended in compromise, including some degree of state support for confessional schools. Religion no longer barred access to jobs, education or political power. As early as the 1890s English political Nonconformity was being crushed by the weight of its own success; by the 1960s the same was true of the political Catholicism of countries like Belgium and the Netherlands. The various forms of discrimination and persecution had been overcome. Now the ghettos were beginning to feel claustrophobic. The secularising effect of a pluralist society lay primarily in the fact that the religious community was ceasing to be a necessary source of identity and support, and that neighbours who had once been regarded largely in terms of hostile stereotypes could now be seen as offering alternative ways of living.

At the same time, the affluence of the 1950s and 1960s tended to undermine those forms of religion and irreligion that had their main roots in the group life of a community defined by social class, political allegiance or sectarian identity. Rapidly increasing incomes for most sections of the west-European population; easier credit facilities; decreased dependence on neighbours, kin, or mutual aid organisations; greater mobility: all of these tended to focus life on the home and the nuclear family. Husband and wife were increasingly tending to do things together, and very often to do them at home. One facet of this situation was the domination of leisure by the car and the television set: a survey in London in the early 1970s found that men and women in their thirties and forties spent an average of two hours a day watching television. Another was the rising level of home ownership, and the tendency for the home to become the major source of identity and satisfaction for its members.[13] In the earlier twentieth century the home-centred life of groups like the British lower middle class had its rationale in the ethos of respectability, which had the effect of maintaining a common value-system and a strong sense of social identity within the most apparently individualistic sections of society. By the 1960s, this ethos was declining in the face of ideals of freedom and individual self-fulfilment. It is probably the weakening of communal ties which explains the increasing volatility of voting patterns in the late 1960s and 1970s. Not only the sectarian base of the Dutch Catholic People's Party, but the class base of the British Labour Party was being undermined: the predictions of the 1950s that prosperity would turn working-class voters into middle-class Conservatives were wrong; but the most recent evidence suggests that there are an increasing number of mainly pragmatic voters, with little sense of political identity.[14]

In this situation those churches that had bound together whole communities were in decline. The religious movements that were flourishing had a sectarian character: their membership was small, but highly active, and to some degree insulated from direct contact with the unbelieving world. A typical example would be the house church movement, which grew rapidly in Britain in the 1970s, and was so called because it consisted of small groups meeting initially in private houses, usually following a split in an Anglican, Baptist, Methodist or Brethren congregation. These splits arose from differing reactions to the 'charismatic renewal' movement which began in the 1960s and proved a considerable source both of inspiration and division mainly among evangelical Protestants, but also among other Christian groups, notably Roman Catholics. The main focus of this movement was the experience of the 'baptism of the Holy Spirit', usually followed by speaking in tongues, and manifested in a variety of spiritual gifts, including the ability to prophesy and to heal the sick. Many of the new congregations soon attracted enough adherents to require larger premises, though even when they met in a hired hall or in their own building on Sunday, there continued to be frequent small-scale gatherings on week-nights. By 1979 leaders estimated that 40 per cent of members had no previous church commitment. The attractions of these churches include lively and informal worship, a tight-knit and strongly supportive community, and a distinctive and highly ordered life-style. Strict discipline and a very heavy programme of church activities help to prevent members from falling under rival influences.[15] Organisations of Christians on the 'house church' model were seen in many other countries in the later 1960s and early 1970s, though the actual content of their Christianity differed widely. Both among Dutch and Spanish Catholics and among East German Protestants there was a proliferation of small groups of lay Christians, using experimental forms of worship, and sometimes seeing radical political objectives as an essential part of their faith. In East

Germany the trend towards meeting in small groups with lay leaders in private houses has been made necessary by the shortage of clergy or church buildings. In Spain and the Netherlands such groups have often had their origins in clashes with the church authorities, and have sometimes been led by an ex-priest.

The religious trend of the late 1960s and early 1970s seemed to be epitomised by Amsterdam: a large part of the population declared themselves of 'no religion' (52 per cent according to the 1972 census), and there were no very great differences between the classes in the size of the 'non-religious' element (working class highest with 57 per cent, professionals and white-collar class lowest with 45 per cent). Surveys suggested that many of the 'non-religious' had supernaturalist beliefs, often of a Christian kind: 'no religion' primarily meant a rejection of the churches. The national church had suffered a catastrophic decline since the start of this century, and now attracted only about 20 per cent even of the church-going population. There were also large numbers of small, and in relation to the wider society, highly eccentric, religious groupings. A brief survey of the 'religious sub-culture' of the city in the early 1970s placed these in four main categories: politically active radical Christians, living on the margins of the orthodox churches; fundamentalist Protestants, most notably Jehovah's Witnesses, but more recently including groups like the Children of God, appealing explicitly to the young; groups inspired by eastern religious ideas; and 'syncretist' movements, notably the Unification Church. However, the membership of these movements made up a small proportion of the total population, and they were probably outnumbered by the adherents of the Marxist sub-culture, who shared with them 'a messianic ideology, aimed at ending the alienation of man in an industrial culture'.[16]

As the nineteenth century and the first half of the twentieth had been a period of religious polarisation, the 1960s appeared to be a time of religious fragmentation. The social supports for religious commitment were weakening, and religious organisations were increasingly dependent on the more erratic basis of personal commitment. Even the most 'church'-like religious institutions were taking on a more sectarian character, and explicitly sectarian movements were an increasingly prominent part of the religious landscape. But where the 'churches' and 'sects' of the nineteenth century were often deeply rooted in a particular social milieu, and were closely identified with the style of life and the political demands of a whole class, in the 1960s all religious movements were tending to become the province of committed minorities, to some degree eccentric within their own social environment.

Notes

Chapter 1

Place of publication is London, unless stated otherwise.

1. M. Reinhard, *Paris pendant la Révolution*, 2 vols., Paris, 1966, I, p.196.

2. Y.-G. Paillard, 'Fanatiques et patriotes dans le Puy-de-Dôme', *Annales Historiques de la Révolution Française*, no. 233, juillet-septembre 1978, p.377.

3. O. Hufton, 'Women in Revolution 1789–1796', *Past & Present*, no. 53, November 1971, p.107.

4. G. Cholvy, 'Religion et révolution: la déchristianisation de l'an II', *Annales Historiques de la Révolution Française*, no. 233, juillet-septembre 1978, p.461.

5. T.J.A. Le Goff and D.M.G. Sutherland, 'The Revolution and the rural community in eighteenth-century Brittany', *Past & Present*, no. 62, February 1974, p.116.

6. B. Plongeron, *Conscience religieuse en révolution*, Paris, 1969, pp.154–71.

7. Ibid., loc. cit.

8. M. Vovelle, *Piété baroque et déchristianisation en Provence au XVIIIe siècle*, Paris, 1973, pp.326–7.

9. R. Cobb, *Les armées révolutionnaires*, 2 vols., Paris, 1961–3, II, pp.646–7.

10. A. Soboul, *Les sans-culottes parisiens en l'an II*, Paris, 1958, p.283.

11. A. Soboul, *Paysans, sans-culottes et jacobins*, Paris, 1966, pp.183–98.

12. Soboul, *Les sans-culottes parisiens*, pp.285–6; J. Bernet, 'Les origines de la déchristianisation dans le district de Compiègne', *Annales Historiques de la Révolution Française*, no. 233, juillet-septembre 1978, p.410.

13. Cobb, op.cit., II, p.647.

14. G. Cholvy, *Religion et société au XIXe siècle: Le diocèse de Montpellier*. 2 vols., Lille, 1973, I, p.136; M. Lagrée, *Mentalités, religion et histoire en Haute Bretagne au XIXe siècle*, Paris, 1977, pp.79–83.

15. Cholvy, op.cit., I, pp.86–7.

16. C.A. Macartney, *The social Revolution in Austria*, Cambridge, 1926, p.54.

17. J.M. Vazquez, *Así viven y mueren*, Madrid, 1958, p.56.

18. B. Harrison and B. Trinder, 'Drink and Sobriety in an early Victorian Country Town: Banbury, 1830–60', *English Historical Review*, Special Supplement, no.4, 1969; B. Trinder, 'The Economy of Banbury, c.1830–70',

paper read to Birmingham University Social History Seminar, December 1978.

19. E. Kossmann, *The Low Countries, 1780–1940*, Oxford, 1978, p.569.

20. M.R. Lepsius. 'Parteiensystem und Sozialstruktur', G. Ritter (ed.), *Deutsche Parteien vor 1918*, Cologne, 1973, pp.56–81.

21. J. Newsinger, 'Revolution and Catholicism in Ireland, 1848–1923', *European Studies Review*, IX, 4, October 1979, p.463.

Chapter 2

1. Y.-M. Hilaire, *Une chrétienté au XIXe siècle? La vie religieuse des populations du diocèse d'Arras, 1840–1914*, 2 vols., Lille, 1977, II, pp.636–46.

2. See, e.g., Archbishop Benson's comments on his nomination of a socialist to a vacant living in Lambeth in 1891. P.d'A. Jones, *The Christian Socialist Revival, 1877–1914*, Princeton, 1968, p.246.

3. F. Isambert, *Christianisme et classe ouvrière*, Tournai, 1961, p.74.

4. P. Drews, *Das kirchliche Leben der Evangelisch-Lutherischen Landeskirche des Königreichs Sachsen*, Tübingen, 1902, p.365.

5. J. Pitt-Rivers, *People of the Sierras*, 1954, p.133.

6. H. Gurdon, 'The Methodist Parish Chest', *History Workshop Journal*, no.3, Spring 1977, p.75; information from Dorothy Graham, who is doing research at Birmingham University on women preachers in early Primitive Methodism.

7. E. Isichei, *Victorian Quakers*, 1970, pp.94–5, 107–9.

8. M. Marrus, 'Pilger auf dem Weg: Wallfahrten im Frankreich des 19. Jahrhunderts', *Geschichte und Gesellschaft*, III, 3, 1977, pp.342–3.

9. J. Obelkevich, *Religion and rural Society: South Lindsey, 1825–1875*, Oxford, 1976, pp.149–50, 313; R. Marbach, *Säkularisierung und sozialer Wandel im 19.Jahrhundert*, Göttingen, 1978, pp.46–50.

10. Obelkevich, op.cit., p.53.

11. F. Le Play, *Les Ouvriers européens*, 6 vols., Tours, 1877, VI, p.157.

12. L.S. Strumingher, '"A bas les prêtres! A bas les couvents!": The Church and the Workers in nineteenth-century Lyon', *Journal of Social History*, XI, 4, Summer 1978, pp.546–7.

13. R. Moore, *Pit-men, Politics and Preachers*, 1974, p.146.

14. T. Zeldin, 'The Conflict of Moralities', Zeldin (ed.), *Conflicts in French Society*, 1970, p.49; Y.-M. Hilaire, 'La pratique religieuse en France de 1815 à 1878', *L'Information Historique*, XXV, 1963, p.64.

15. T. Zeldin, *France, 1848–1945*, 2 vols., Oxford, 1973–7, I, p.308.

16. Pitt-Rivers, op.cit., pp.90, 113; C. Lison-Tolosona, *Belmonte de los Caballeros*, Oxford, 1966, ch.13.

17. Zeldin, *France, 1848–1945*, I, pp.300,293; J. Pataut, *Sociologie électorale de la Nièvre au XXe Siècle*, as quoted in G. Dupeux, *French Society, 1789–1970*, English translation, 1976, p.186.

Chapter 3

1. F. Vanden Berg, *Abraham Kuyper*, Grand Rapids, 1960, pp.37–8.

2. A.D. Gilbert, *Religion and Society in industrial England, 1740–1914*, 1976, pp.63,67.

3. J. Rule, 'The labouring Miner in Cornwall, c.1740–1870', Warwick University Ph.D. thesis, 1971, pp.240–60.

4. J. Hunter, *The Making of the Crofting Community*, Edinburgh, 1976, p.101.

5. R. Colls, *The Collier's Rant*, 1977, p.78.

6. Moore, op.cit., p.142.

7. H.U. Faulkner, *Chartism and the Churches*, New York, 1916, p.53; Colls, op.cit., p.101.

8. B. Harrison, *Drink and the Victorians*, 1971, pp.117–8.

9. Obelkevich, op.cit., p.102.

10. J. Briggs and I. Sellers, *Victorian Nonconformity*, 1973, pp.62–3.

11. O. Anderson, 'The Incidence of Civil Marriage in Victorian England and Wales', *Past & Present*, no.69, Nov. 1975, p.76; E.T. Davies, *Religion in the Industrial Revolution in South Wales*, Cardiff, 1965, p.49.

12. H. Snell, *Men, Movements and Myself*, 1936, p.33.

13. Harrison and Trinder, op.cit., pp.40–6.

14. Information from John Fletcher, who has recorded an interview with an elderly villager who had watched the skimmington.

15. G. Brenan, *The Spanish Labyrinth*, 2nd ed., 1950, pp.207–8.

16. B. Singer, 'The Village Schoolmaster as Outsider', J. Beauroy and others (eds.), *The Wolf and the Lamb: Popular Culture in France from the Ancien Régime to the twentieth Century*, Saratoga, 1977, pp.189–208.

17. P. Göhre, *Three Months in a Workshop*, English translation, 1895, pp.108–9.

18. Ibid., pp.111–43.

19. Ibid., pp.76–7, 210.

20. E. Schwiedland, *Kleingewerbe und Hausindustrie in Österreich*, 2 vols., Leipzig, 1894, II, pp.269–85.

21. J.M. Mayeur, 'Mgr Dupanloup et Louis Veuillot devant les "prophéties contemporaines" en 1874', *Revue d'Histoire de la Spiritualité*, XLVIII, 1972, pp.193–204.

22. Hilaire, op.cit., I, p.395; Cholvy, op.cit., II, pp.1422–8.

23. Marrus, op.cit., p.351.

24. F. Lannon, 'The socio-political Role of the Spanish Church – A Case-Study', *Journal of Contemporary History*, XIV, April 1979, p.199.

25. E. Larkin, 'The devotional Revolution in Ireland, 1850–75', *American Historical Review*, LXXVII, 3 July 1972, pp.622–52.

26. J. Mather, 'The Assumptionist Response to Secularisation, 1870–1900', R. Bezucha (ed.), *Modern European Social History*, Lexington, 1971, pp.59–89.

27. K. Tenfelde, *Sozialgeschichte der Bergarbeiterschaft an der Ruhr im 19. Jahrhundert*, Bonn, 1977, pp.386–96; H. Grote, *Sozialdemokratie und Religion*, Tübingen, 1968, p.189; V.L. Lidtke, 'Die kulturelle Bedeutung der Arbeitervereine', G. Wiegelmann (ed.). Kulturaller Wandel im 19.Jahrhundert, Göttingen, 1973, pp.146–8, 153–4; E. Weber, 'Gymnastics and Sports in fin-de-siècle France: The Opium of the Classes?', *American Historical Review*, LXXVI, 1, Feb. 1971, p.93.

28. Mather, op.cit., p.60.

29. F. Lannon, 'Catholic Bilbao from Restoration to Republic: A selective Study of educational Institutions', Oxford University D.Phil. thesis, 1975, pp.163–4, 183–94.

Chapter 4

1. H. Mendras, *Sociologie de la campagne française*, Paris, 1959, pp.75–6.

2. A. Chatelain, *Les migrants temporaires en France de 1800 à 1914*, 2 vols., Villeneuve d'Ascq, 1976, II, p.1099.

3. Obelkevich, op.cit., pp.2–6; Hilaire, op.cit., I, pp.34–5, II, p.567.

4. G. Cholvy, 'Expressions et évolution du sentiment religieux populaire dans la France du XIXe siècle au temps de la restauration catholique (1801–60)', *Actes du 99e Congrès National des Sociétés Savantes*, Paris, 1976, I, p.296.

5. W. Brepohl, *Industrievolk im Wandel von der agraren zur industriellen Daseinsform dargestellt am Ruhrgebiet*, Tübingen, 1957, p.285.

6. Drews, op.cit., p.90; Cholvy, *Religion et société*, I, pp.49–54.

7. Hunter, op.cit., p.94.

8. Davies, op.cit., pp.115–9; Hunter, op.cit., p.94; D.W. Miller, 'Irish Catholicism and the Great Famine', *Journal of Social History*, IX, 1, Fall 1975, pp.83–8; C. Langlois, *Un diocèse breton au début du XIX siècle*, Rennes, 1974, pp.473–4.

9. Le Play, op.cit., IV, pp.88–92.

10. O. Hufton, *The Poor of eighteenth-century France*, Oxford, 1976, pp.349–51; P.M. Jones, 'Parish, Seigneurie and Community of Inhabitants', forthcoming in *Past & Present*.

11. J. Delumeau, *Le catholicisme entre Luther et Voltaire*, Paris, 1971, pp.206–7.

12. Marbach, op.cit., pp.38–9; Drews, op.cit., pp.354–5, 364–5.

13. Obelkevich, op.cit., p.155; D.M. Thompson, 'The Churches and Society in nineteenth-century England: A rural Perspective,' G.J. Cuming and D. Baker (eds.), *Studies in Church History, 8*, 1972, p.269.

14. F. Thompson, *Lark Rise to Candleford*, 1954, pp.6,335–6.

15. Cholvy, *Religion et société*, I, p.86; H. Thomas, *The Spanish Civil War*, Harmondsworth, 1965, p.29.

16. M. Agulhon, *La république au village*, Paris, 1970, pp.174–8.

17. R. Braun, *Industrialisierung und Volksleben*, Zurich, 1960, p.134; P. Wurster,

Das kirchliche Leben der evangelischen Landeskirche in Württemberg, Tübingen, 1919, p.114.

18. Obelkevich, op.cit., pp.274–6, 287,302.

19. Drews, op.cit., pp.349–50.

20. P. Joutard, 'Protestantisme populaire et univers magique: Le cas cevenol', *Le Monde Alpin et Rhodanien*, 1977, p.168. There is extensive evidence of the same phenomenon in religiously mixed areas of Germany in the article on 'Konfession' in E. Hoffman-Krayer (ed.), *Handwörterbuch des deutschen Aberglaubens*, 9 vols., Berlin, 1927–38.

21. S. Bonnet, 'Les "sauvages" de Futeau, verriers et bûcherons d'Argonne aux XVIIIe et XIXe siècles', F. Bédarida & J. Maitron (eds.), *Christianisme et monde ouvrier*, Paris, 1975, pp.196, 206–7, 219–20.

22. G. Cholvy, 'La France contemporaine (XIXe-début XXe siècles)', B. Plongeron (ed.), *La religion populaire dans l'occident chrétien*, Paris, 1976, pp.160–1.

23. This paragraph is mainly based on an unpublished paper on church orchestras by John Fletcher.

24. Rule, op.cit., pp.304–7.

25. Hilaire, op.cit., II, p.575.

26. G. Bourne, *Change in the Village*, 1912, p.295.

27. J. Cutileiro, *A Portuguese Rural Society*, Oxford, 1971, pp.23–4,262–8; Pitt-Rivers, op.cit., pp.68, 132–3; W.A. Christian, *Person and God in a Spanish Valley*, New York, 1972.

28. J.P. Kruijt, 'Die Erforschung der protestantischen Kirchengemeinde in den Niederlanden', D. Goldschmidt and others (eds.), *Soziologie der Kirchengemeinde*, Stuttgart, 1960, p.36.

29. See, e.g., R. Fraser, *The Pueblo: A Mountain Village on the Costa del Sol*, 1973, pp.51–7 (interview with Anarchist shoemaker); E.J. Hobsbawm, *Primitive Rebels*, 2nd ed., Manchester, 1971, pp.184–5 (interview with Communist shoemaker in southern Italy).

30. R. Luneau, 'Monde rural et christianisation: prêtres et paysans français du siècle dernier,' *Archives des Sciences Sociales de la Religion*, 43/1, janvier-mars 1977, p.46.

31. E. Weber, *Peasants into Frenchmen*, 1977, pp.339–74, 389–90, 446–70.

32. There is a fairly similar picture of religious change in L. Wylie, *Chanzeaux, A Village in Anjou*, Cambridge, Mass., 1966, ch. 13 and *passim*.

33. Zeldin, *France, 1848–1945*, I, p.193; S. Berger, *Peasants against Politics: Rural Organisation in Brittany 1911–67*, Cambridge, Mass., 1972; G. Lewis, 'The Peasantry, rural Change and conservative Agrarianism: Lower Austria at the Turn of the Century', *Past & Present*, no.81, Nov. 1978, pp.119–43; R. Fraser, *Blood of Spain*, 1979, pp.83–6.

34. G. Cholvy, *Géographie religieuse de l'Hérault contemporain*, Paris, 1968, pp. 471–6 G. Cholvy, 'Le catholicisme en Rouergue aux XIXe et XXe siècles:

Première approche', *Actes du Congrès d'Etudes de Rodez*, Rodez, 1975, pp.264–7.

Chapter 5

1. L. Wirth, 'Urbanism as a Way of Life', *American Journal of Sociology*, XLIV, 1938–9, pp.1–24. *Grenouilles* (frogs) was the French Catholic term for Protestants, and *Schwarzen* (blacks) the German Protestant term for Catholics.

2. Paul Thompson and Thea Vigne's Interviews on Family Life and Work Experience before 1918, University of Essex, no.261, pp.41–2.

3. H. McLeod, 'White Collar Values and the Role of Religion', G. Crossick (ed.), *The Lower Middle Class in Britain, 1870–1914*, 1977, p.74.

4. S. Baker, 'Orange and Green: Belfast, 1832–1914', H.J. Dyos and M.Wolff (eds.), *The Victorian City*, 2 vols., 1973, II, p.804.

5. H. Perkin, *The Origins of Modern English Society, 1780–1880*, 1969, p.289; E.P. Thompson, *The Making of the English Working Class*, 2nd ed., Harmondsworth, 1968, pp.451,456–69.

6. Moore, op.cit., pp.140–52.

7. G. Acorn, *One of the Multitude*, 1911, pp.1–8,51,149–51.

8. L. Lees, *Exiles of Erin: Irish Migrants in Victorian London*, Manchester, 1979, pp.207–12; Booth Collection (London School of Economics Library) B180, p.13, B265, pp.131–3.

9. Thompson and Vigne's Interviews, op.cit. nos.245,232,54.

10. R. Tressell, *The Ragged Trousered Philanthropists*, 1965 [1st ed., 1914], p.453.

11. G. Robson, 'Between Town and Countryside: Contrasting Patterns of Churchgoing in the early Victorian Black Country', D. Baker (ed.), *Studies in Church History, 15*, Oxford, 1979, pp.409–10.

12. P. Guiral, 'Marseille', L. Chevalier (ed.), *Le Choléra*, La Roche-sur-Yon, 1958, pp.136–9.

13. L. Chevalier, *Labouring Classes and Dangerous Classes in Paris during the first Half of the nineteenth Century*, English translation, 1973, pp.13–17; Brenan, op.cit., p.43.

14. Wurster, op.cit., p.87.

15. Drews, op.cit., p.90.

16. C. Tilly, *The Vendée*, 1964, pp.186–92,260–2, and *passim*.

17. Y. Le Gallo, *Brest et sa bourgeoisie sous la Monarchie de Juillet*, Paris, 1968, pp.45–7.

18. D. Higgs, 'The Portuguese Church', W.J. Callahan and D. Higgs (eds.), *Church and Society in Catholic Europe of the eighteenth Century*, Cambridge, 1979, pp.54–5; Reinhard, op.cit., I, pp.199–207,256–8.

19. O. Hufton, 'The French Church', Callahan and Higgs (eds.), op.cit., p.29.

20. F. Houtart, *Les paroisses de Bruxelles, 1803–1951*, Brussels, 1955; Y. Daniel,

L'équipement paroissial d'un diocèse urbain (Paris, 1802–1956), Paris, 1957.

21. T.H.S. Escott, *Society in London*, 1885, pp.162–3.

22. M. Young and P. Willmott, *Family and Kinship in East London*, Harmondsworth, 1962, p.112; R. Roberts, *The Classic Slum*, Manchester, 1971, pp.3–4; P.H. Chombert de Lauwe, *Paris et l'agglomération parisienne*, 2 vols., Paris, 1952, I, p.57.

23. W. Köllmann, *Sozialgeschichte der Stadt Barmen im 19.Jahrhundert*, Tübingen, 1960, p.206; P. Pierrard, *La vie ouvrière à Lille sous le Second Empire*, Paris, 1965, p.415; H. McLeod, *Class and Religion in the late Victorian City*, 1974, p.71.

24. W.H. Reid, *The Rise and Dissolution of the Infidel Societies of the Metropolis*, 1800, pp.18–21.

25. K. Busia, *Urban Churches in Britain*, 1966, pp.22–3, 153; G.K. Nelson, 'Religious Groups in a changing social Environment', A. Bryman (ed.), *Religion in the Birmingham Area*, Birmingham, 1975, p.59.

26. St. C. Drake and H. Cayton, *Black Metropolis*, rev. ed., New York, 1970, p.653.

27. F. Schnabel, *Deutsche Geschichte im 19.Jahrhundert: Die protestantischen Kirchen in Deutschland*, Freiburg, 1965, pp.355–6; H. Freudenthal, *Vereine in Hamburg*, Hamburg, 1968; Wurster, op.cit. pp.229–32; Drews, op.cit., pp.89–92.

28. McLeod, *Class and Religion*, pp.113–14,135,139–40,220–1, 235–7.

29. Marrus, op.cit., pp.345,350.

30. G.K. Nelson, *Spiritualism and Society*, 1969, pp.155–7; A. Wilkinson, *The Church of England and the First World War*, 1978, ch.7–8; D.S. Cairns (ed.), *The Army and Religion*, 1919, pp.9,172–7.

31. H. Freimark, *Moderne Geisterbeschwörer und Wahrheitssucher*, Grossstadt-Dokumente, XXXVIII, Berlin, n.d., p.51; E. Pin, *Pratique religieuse et classes sociales*, Paris, 1956, pp.400–1.

32. G. Gorer, *Exploring English Character*, 1955, p.269; N. Abercrombie and others, 'Superstition and Religion: The God of the Gaps', D. Martin and M. Hill (eds.), *Sociological Yearbook of Religion in Britain*, 3, 1970, pp.93–129.

33. D. Bonhöffer, *Letters and Papers from Prison*, English translation, 1959, p.91.

34. S. Laury, 'Aspects de la pratique religieuse dans le diocèse d'Arras (1919 –45)', *Revue du Nord*, no.208, janvier-mars 1971, p.126.

Chapter 6

1. *Das fröhliche Wissenschàft*, paragraph 108.

2. *Jenseits von Gut und Böse* (1886), reprinted in F. Nietzsche, *Werke*, 3 vols., Munich, 1955, II, pp.618–9.

3. Drews, op.cit., pp.365–6; Wurster, op.cit., pp.85,88; W. Wendland, *700 Jahre Kirchengeschichte Berlins*, Berlin, 1930, pp.288, 302–3,330.

4. H.H. Gerth and C. Wright Mills (eds.), *From Max Weber*, 1948, p.139 (from Weber's speech on 'Science as a Vocation,' Munich University, 1918).

5. S. Patten, *The new Basis of Civilisation*, as quoted in W.L. O'Neill, *Divorce in the Progressive Era*, New Haven, 1967, p.163.

6. Drews, op.cit., pp.366–7; Wendland, op.cit., pp.309–16,335–41.

7. R. Stadelmann and W. Fischer, *Die Bildungswelt des deutschen Handwerkers um 1800*, Berlin, 1955, pp.180–1.

8. P. Pieper, *Kirchliche Statistik Deutschlands*, Freiburg, 1899, p.232. For church attendance counts or estimates see ibid., pp.238–9; Wendland, op.cit., pp.309–16; Wurster, op.cit., p.85. These suggest an average Sunday attendance by 6 per cent of state church Protestants in Hanover and 5 per cent in Ulm around the turn of the century, and of 2 per cent at Sunday *morning* services in Berlin in 1869.

9. A. Briggs, 'Middle Class Consciousness in English Politics, 1780–1846', *Past & Present*, no.9, April 1956, pp.85–93.

10. Langlois, op.cit., p.475.

11. Cholvy, *Religion et société*, I, p.590; A. Daumard, *La bourgeoisie parisienne de 1815 à 1848*, Paris, 1964, pp.347–51,366–8,617–23.

12. E. Poulat, 'Déchristianisation du prolétariat ou dépérissement de la religion?', Bédarida and Maitron (eds.), op.cit., pp.67–73.

13. P. Droulers, 'Catholicisme et mouvement ouvrier en France au XIXe siècle: L'attitude de l'épiscopat', ibid., pp.54–5.

14. Cholvy, *Religion et société*, II, p.1441.

15. *Quarterly Review*, cxliii, May 1843, pp.232–3.

16. H. Taine, *Notes on England*, English translation, 1957, pp.11–12,96,116,192.

17. B.M. Ratcliffe and W.H. Chaloner (eds.), *A French Sociologist looks at Britain: Gustave d'Eichthal and British Society in 1828*, Manchester, 1977, pp.78–9.

18. V. Kiernan 'Evangelicalism and the French Revolution', *Past & Present*, no. 1, February 1952, pp.46–50.

19. B.I. Coleman, 'The Church Extension Movement in London, c.1800–60', Cambridge University Ph.D. thesis, 1968, pp.21–2,308–13.

20. R. Balgarnie, *Sir Titus Salt, Baronet, His Life and its Lessons*, 1877, pp.80–5.

21. A. Briggs, *Victorian People*, Harmondsworth, 1965, p.129.

22. A. MacLaren, *Religion and Social Class: The Disruption Years in Aberdeen*, 1974, p.182.

23. Moore, op.cit., pp.78–92, 155–68.

24. Ibid., pp.90–1; S. Yeo, *Religion and Voluntary Organisations in Crisis*, 1976, pp.106–7.

25. A. Gustafson, *A History of Swedish Literature*, 1960, as quoted by R.F. Tomasson, *Sweden: Prototype of modern Society*, New York, 1970, p.288.

26. *The Works of Bernard Shaw*, 1930, XIX, p.38.

27. G. Allen, 'The New Hedonism', *Fortnightly Review*, New Series, CCCXXVII,

March 1, 1894, pp.379–80.

28. McLeod, *Class and Religion*, p.238.

29. E.g., the fathers of Kingsley Amis and James Kenward, both born in south London middle-class families in the late nineteenth century: J. Kenward, *The Suburban Child*, 1955, pp.26–39; K. Amis, *What became of Jane Austen?*, 1970, p.192.

30. Pin, op.cit.; J. Freytag and K. Ozaki, *Nominal Christianity: Studies of Church and People in Hamburg*, English translation, 1970.

Chapter 7

1. B. Gustafsson, *Socialdemokratien och kyrkan, 1881–90*, Stockholm, 1953, English summary.

2. Schwiedland, op.cit., II, p.265.

3. C.S. Davies, *North Country Bred*, 1963, pp.100,116.

4. Gerth and Mills (eds.), op.cit., pp.275–6; Pin, op.cit., p.275.

5. A. Popp, *Die Jugendgeschichte einer Arbeiterin*, 3rd ed., Munich, 1927, p,55.

6. Acorn, op.cit., pp.50–1.

7. Houtart, op.cit., pp.55–8.

8. Köllmann, op.cit., pp.150–3,198–212.

9. R.F Hamilton, *Affluence and the French Worker in the Fourth Republic*, Princeton, 1967, p.268.

10. Interview with Wesley Perrins, *Bulletin of the Society for the Study of Labour History*, no.21, Autumn 1970, pp.16–24.

11. Hobsbawm, op.cit., pp.142–5.

12. Drews, op.cit., pp.354–5; Hamilton, op.cit., pp.268–9.

13. R. Hoggart, *The Uses of Literacy*, 1957, ch.2–5.

14. To quote the well-known music-hall song used by Gareth Stedman Jones in his fine essay, 'Working Class Culture and Working Class Politics in London, 1870–1900', *Journal of Social History*, VII, 4, Summer 1974, p.118.

15. A.E.C.W. Spencer, 'The Demography and Sociography of the Roman Catholic Community in England and Wales', L. Bright and S. Clements (eds.). *The Committed Church*, 1965, p.78.

16. J. Bossy, *The English Catholic Community, 1570–1850*, 1976, p.353.

17. S.W. Gilley, 'Evangelical and Roman Catholic Missions to the Irish in London, 1830–70', University of Cambridge Ph.D. thesis, 1971, pp.375–6.

18. *The Rambler*, IV, 1849, p.434, as quoted by S.W. Gilley, 'The Roman Catholic Mission to the Irish in London', *Recusant History*, X, 3, October, 1969, p.145.

19. S. Gilley, 'Catholic Faith of the Irish Slums: London, 1840–70', Dyos and Wolff (eds.), op.cit., II, p.839.

Chapter 8

1. T. Luckmann, *The invisible Religion*, English translation, New York, 1967, pp.36–9.

2. E. Aver and others, 'Pratique religieuse et comportement électoral', *Archives de Sociologie des Religions*, no.29, janvier-juin 1970, pp.27–52; R.E.M. Irving, *The Christian Democratic Parties of western Europe*, 1979, p.167; J.A. Coleman, *The Evolution of Dutch Catholicism, 1958–74*, Los Angeles, 1978, pp.69,72–3.

3. Quoted in Tomasson, op.cit., p.85.

4. P. Salomonsen, 'Contemporary religious Attitudes in Denmark – A qualitative Description based on empirical Research', *Acts of the 12th International Conference on the Sociology of Religion*, Lille, 1973, p.454.

5. K. Coates and R. Silburn, *Poverty: The forgotten Englishmen*, Harmondsworth, 1970, pp.113–4.

6. G. Richman, *Fly a Flag for Poplar*, n.d., pp.44,88,97.

7. B. Wilhelm, 'Germany: Democratic Republic', H.Mol (ed.), *Western Religion*, The Hague, 1972, p.214.

8. *Social Compass*, XXI, 2, 1974, special number on Soviet sociology of religion.

9. T. Beeson, *Discretion and Valour*, 1974, pp.167–89; Wilhelm, op.cit., pp.213 –28; Pastorin Christa Grengel, Cadbury Lectures, University of Birmingham, 1975.

10. Speech to the conference of the West German Green Party, translated in *New Statesman*, January 18, 1980.

11. R. Duocastella-Rosell, 'Espagne, société et église en processus de change-ment', *12th Conference on Sociology of Religion*, p.198.

12. R. Duocastella, *Sociología y pastoral del turismo en la Costa Brava y Maresme*, Madrid, 1969, ch.15.

13. M. Young and P. Willmott, *The Symmetrical Family*, 1973, pp.98–100,213, and *passim*.

14. D. Butler & D. Stokes, *Political Change in Britain*, 2nd ed., 1974, ch.9.

15. J.V. Thurman, 'New Wine Skins: A Study of the House Church Movement', University of Birmingham M.A. thesis, 1979.

16. T. Nuij, 'La subculture religieuse de la ville d'Amsterdam', *12th Conference on Sociology of Religion*, pp.377–91; L. Laeyendecker, 'The Netherlands,' Mol (ed.), op.cit., pp.340–1.

Further Reading

General

Four wide-ranging interpretations of the religious history of this period, each of which covers some of the same ground as this book, although their overall approaches are very different, are: Owen Chadwick, *The Secularisation of the European Mind*, Cambridge, 1975; David Martin, *A General Theory of Secularisation*, Oxford, 1978; W.R. Ward, *Religion and Society in England 1790–1850*, 1972; A.D. Gilbert, *Religion and Society in Industrial England: Church, Chapel and Social Change, 1740–1914*, 1976. The fairly numerous church histories of the period tend to take little interest in the religion of the mass of the people, and the general histories take little interest in religion at all. However, Eric Hobsbawm's *The Age of Revolution*, 1962, includes an original and stimulating chapter on 'Ideology: Religion'. Also recommended are John Walsh's chapter in vol. IX of the *New Cambridge Modern History* (covering the years 1793–1830), and Peter Burke's bird's eye view of 'Religion and Secularisation' in the *Companion Volume* of the *N.C.M.H.* of which he is also the editor. There is a critical bibliography of modern church history by John Kent in J. Daniélou, A.H. Couratin, J. Kent, *Penguin Guide to Modern Theology, II*, Harmondsworth, 1969. Martin's book includes an extensive list of writing on the contemporary religious situation.

Chapter 1

For religion in the French Revolution the two best books in English are John McManners' brilliant short history, *The French Revolution and the Church*, 1969, and Charles Tilly, *The Vendée* 1964, an intensive local study that draws wide-ranging conclusions. The standard history is A. Latreille, *L'Eglise catholique et la Révolution française*, 2 vols., Paris, 1946–50; the most recent synthesis, concerned mainly with dechristianisation, is M. Vovelle, *Religion et révolution*, Paris, 1976. I have drawn heavily on the work of Richard Cobb, especially *Les armées révolutionnaires*, 2 vols., Paris, 1961–3; also on the chapter on revolutionary cults in A. Soboul, *Paysans, sans-culottes et jacobins*, Paris, 1966; M. Vovelle, *Les métamorphoses de la fête en Provence, 1750–1820*, Paris, 1976; the early chapters of G. Cholvy, *Religion et société au XIXe siècle: Le diocèse de Montpellier*, 2 vols., Lille, 1973; and the special number on dechristianisation of *Annales Historiques de la Révolution Française*, no. 233, juillet-septembre 1978. For French Catholicism on the eve of the Revolution two good guides are the later chapters of J. Delumeau, *Catholicism from Luther to Voltaire*, English translation, 1978, and O. Hufton, 'The French Church', in the valuable symposium, W.J. Callahan and D. Higgs (eds.),

Church and Society in Catholic Europe of the eighteenth Century, Cambridge, 1979, pp.13–33.

The literature on the inter-penetration of religion and politics in the nineteenth and earlier twentieth century is very extensive. Useful attempts at synthesis include A. Dansette, *Religious History of modern France*, 2 vols., English translation, New York, 1962; J. McManners, *Church and State in France, 1870–1914*, 1971; E. Royle. *Radical Politics 1790–1900: Religion and Unbelief*, 1971; F. Fischer, 'Der deutsche Protestantismus und die Politik im 19.Jahrhundert,' *Historische Zeitschrift*, CLXXI, 1951, pp.473–518; J.M. Sanchez, *Reform and Reaction: The Politico – Religious Background to the Spanish Civil War*, Chapel Hill, 1964; J. Newsinger, 'Revolution and Catholicism in Ireland; *European Studies Review*, IX, 4, Oct. 1979 pp.457–80. T. Zeldin (ed.), *Conflicts in French Society*, 1970, is a good collection of essays on religion, anti-clericalism and politics in the nineteenth century. G. Lewy, *Religion and Revolution*, 1973, a wide-ranging investigation into the relationship between politics and various kinds of religion, includes case-studies of the French Revolution and Spanish civil war.

Chapter 2

In the first half of this chapter, my general picture of social change in the early nineteenth century draws most heavily on E.P. Thompson, *Making of the English Working Class*, 2nd ed., Harmondsworth, 1968. Some of the most helpful studies of the response to social conflict of the official churches are E.J. Evans, 'Some Reasons for the Growth of English rural Anti-Clericalism, c.1750–1830,' *Past & Present*, no.66, February 1975, pp.84–109; K.S. Inglis, *The Churches and the Working Classes in Victorian England*, 1963 (which covers all religious denominations); Y.-M. Hilaire, *Une chrétienté au XIXe siècle? La vie religieuse des populations du diocèse d'Arras, 1840–1914*, 2 vols., Lille, 1977 (including, besides much else, a useful section on the conflict between socialism and the church in the mining districts); R.M. Bigler, *The Politics of German Protestantism*, Los Angeles, 1972; W.O. Shanahan, *German Protestants face the social Question, 1815–1871*, Notre Dame, 1954; J.C. Ullman, *The Tragic Week: A Study of Anti-Clericalism in Spain, 1875–1912*, Cambridge, Mass., 1968. Studies of church-going statistics, highlighting social class differences: H. McLeod, 'Class, Community and Region: The religious Geography of nineteenth-century England,' M.M. Hill (ed.), *Sociological Yearbook of Religion in Britain*, 6, 1973, pp.29–72; F. Boulard and J. Rémy, *Pratique religieuse urbaine et régions culturelles*, Paris, 1968.

Differences between the religious attitudes of men and women have been little discussed by historians. But there are useful suggestions in T. Zeldin, *France, 1848–1945*, 2 vols., Oxford, 1973–7, (good on religion generally), and in some anthropological studies, e.g. C. Lison-Tolosona, *Belmonte de los Caballeros*, Oxford, 1966. Recently there have been quite a lot of books on the history of women in this period, but few say much about religion. A significant exception is B.G. Sullivan Smith, 'The Women of the Lille Bourgeoisie, 1850–1914', University of Rochester Ph.D. thesis, 1975. For the role of women in millenarian movements, see J.F.C. Harrison, *The Second Coming*, 1979. E. Isichei, *Victorian Quakers*, 1970, includes some discussion of sex-roles within the Society of Friends.

Chapter 3

A wide-ranging introduction to nineteenth-century evangelical movements is W.R. Ward, 'Popular Religion and the Problem of Control,' G.J. Cuming and D. Baker (eds.), *Studies in Church History*, *8*, 1972, pp.237–53. A lively and equally wide-ranging interpretation is J. Kent, *Holding the Fort*, 1978. An outstanding local study is R. Moore, *Pit-men, Politics and Preachers*, 1974. There are good sections on popular evangelicalism in J. Hunter, *The Making of the Crofting Community*, Edinburgh, 1976; R. Colls, *The Collier's Rant*, 1977; J. Rule, 'The Labouring Miner in Cornwall, c.1740–1870', University of Warwick Ph.D. thesis, 1971. More general studies which throw important light on the context of these movements are B. Harrison, *Drink and the Victorians*, 1971; T.W. Laqueur, *Religion and Respectability: Sunday Schools and Working Class Culture, 1780–1850*, New Haven, 1976. For positivism and related movements: D.G. Charlton, *Secular Religions in France, 1815–70*, 1963. For the religious aspect of socialism: S. Yeo, 'A new Life: The Religion of Socialism in Britain, 1883–96', *History Workshop Journal*, no.4, Autumn 1977, pp.5–56. The attitude of socialist leaders to the church in 1903 is discussed in E. Poulat, 'Socialisme et anti-cléricalisme', *Archives de Sociologie des Religions*, no.10, juillet-décembre 1960, pp.109–32. For the socialist sub-culture: G. Roth, *The Social Democrats in Imperial Germany*, Totowa, 1963; V.L. Lidtke, 'Die kulturelle Bedeutung der Arbeitervereine', G. Wiegelmann (ed.), *Kultureller Wandel im 19. Jahrhundert*, Göttingen, 1973, pp.146–59. A good study of a Catholic sub-culture around the same time is F. Lannon, 'Catholic Bilbao from Restoration to Republic: A selective Study of educational Institutions, 1876–1931', University of Oxford, Ph.D.thesis, 1975.

Chapter 4

The two best books in English are J. Obelkevich, *Religion and rural Society: South Lindsey, 1825–75*, Oxford, 1976, and W.A. Christian's anthropological study of a present-day community, *Person and God in a Spanish Valley*, New York, 1972. Among the vast French literature special mention can be made of two books by Christianne Marcilhacy: *Le diocèse d'Orléans au milieu du XIXe siècle: Les hommes et leur mentalités*, Paris, 1964, and *Le diocèse d'Orléans sous l'épiscopat de Mgr Dupanloup*, Paris 1962; and of a synthetic article by Gérard Cholvy, 'Expressions et évolution du sentiment religieux populaire dans la France du XIXe siècle, au temps de la Restauration Catholique, 1801–60', *Actes du 99e Congrès des Sociétés Savantes*, Paris, 1976. There is much relevant material in the special numbers of *Archives des Sciences Sociales des Religions* on popular religion (no.43, janvier-mars 1977), notably P. Sanchis's article on Portuguese pilgrimage sites, and of *Geschichte und Gesellschaft* on social history of religion (III,3,1977), notably by Marrus on French pilgrimages and by G. Korff on the Trier pilgrimage of 1891. I have also got a lot of help from two books by Michael Phayer, *Religion und das gewöhnliche Volk in Bayern in der Zeit von 1750–1850*, Munich, 1970, and *Sexual Liberation and Religion in nineteenth-century Europe*, 1977; from E. Weber, *Peasants into Frenchmen*, 1977; K.H. Connell, *Irish Peasant Society*, 1968; R. Thabault's excellent microcosmic study, *Mon Village*, translated as *Education and Change in a Village Community*, 1971; and from the series on 'Evangelische

Kirchenkunde' edited by Paul Drews in the early twentieth century, which contains much interesting material on German rural religion.

Chapter 5

There have been many studies of religion in specific cities, but few attempts at synthesis – a rare example of the latter being a short paper by John Kent, 'The Role of Religion in the cultural Structure of the later Victorian City', *Transactions of the Royal Historical Society*, 5th series, XXIII, 1973, pp.153–74. Among the best local studies are S. Yeo, *Religion and Voluntary Organisations in Crisis*, 1976 (mainly about Reading), and A.A. MacLaren, *Religion and social Class: The Disruption Years in Aberdeen*, 1974. Others include: E.R. Wickham, *Church and People in an industrial City*, 1957 (Sheffield); F. Charpin, *Pratique religieuse et formation d'une grande ville*, Paris, 1964 (Marseille); H. McLeod, *Class and Religion in the late Victorian City*, 1974 (London). There is also plenty of relevant material in H.J. Dyos and M. Wolff (eds.), *The Victorian City*, 2 vols., 1973, notably papers by Baker, Gilley and Mole on Belfast, London and Birmingham respectively; and there are good sections on religion in W. Köllmann, *Sozialgeschichte der Stadt Barmen im 19.Jahrhundert*, Tübingen, 1960, and P. Pierrard, *La vie ouvrière a Lille sous le Second Empire*, Paris, 1965. See also D. Baker (ed.), *Studies in Church History*, 15, Oxford, 1979, the theme of which is 'the country and the city'. Other works I found especially helpful included: W. Brepohl, *Industrievolk im Wandel von der agraren zur industriellen Daseinsform dargestellt am Ruhrgebiet*, Tübingen, 1957; S. Hickey, 'The Shaping of the German Labour Movement: Miners in the Ruhr', R.J. Evans (ed.), *Society and Politics in Wilhelmine Germany*, 1978, pp.215–40; on Nîmes, G. Lewis, *The Second Vendée*, Oxford, 1978; R. Aminzade 'Class Struggles and Social Change: Toulouse, 1830–72', University of Michigan Ph.D. thesis, 1978.

Chapter 6

There has been much less historical investigation of middle-class religion than of that of other social groups. Among the few specific studies are Clyde Binfield's collection of essays, mainly on middle-class Congregationalism, *So Down to Prayers: Studies in English Nonconformity, 1780–1920*, 1977, and the chapters by R.Q. Gray and H. McLeod in G. Crossick (ed.), *The Lower Middle Class in Britain, 1870–1914*, 1977. More general studies of the middle class with substantial sections on religion include E.P. Hennock, *Fit and Proper Persons*, 1973 (Birmingham's Nonconformist élite); Y. Le Gallo, *Brest et sa bourgoisie sous la Monarchie de Juillet*, 2 vols., Paris, 1968. Histories of religious movements which stress their middle-class roots include I. Bradley, *The Call to Seriousness: The Evangelical Impact on the Victorians*, 1976, and S. Budd, *Varieties of Unbelief: Atheists and Agnostics in English Society, 1850–1960*, 1977, a comprehensive study, that covers both working-class secularism and middle-class rationalism. In this chapter I have drawn most heavily on the studies of urban religion, listed in connection with chapter 5, and on the French diocesan studies, some of which are mentioned in connection with chapters 1 and 4: the former tend to focus mainly on the working class, the latter on the peasants, but most include useful material on other groups.

Chapter 7

For a wide-ranging introduction, see two essays by Eric Hobsbawm: *Primitive Rebels*, Manchester, 1959, ch.8; 'Religion and the Rise of Socialism'. O. Dudley Edwards (ed.), *Humanism and History*, Edinburgh, 1977, pp.9–16. For a summary of the French evidence: F.-A. Isambert, *Christianisme et classe ouvrière*, Tournai, 1961. Two useful interpretations of the nineteenth-century English evidence are J. Kent, 'Feelings and Festivals', Dyos and Wolff (eds.), op.cit., II, pp.655–71; A. Ainsworth, 'Religion in the Working Class Community in Lancashire', *Histoire Sociale*, X, November 1977, pp.354–80. Another stimulating interpretative essay is V.L. Lidtke, 'August Bebel and German Social Democracy's Relation to the Christian Churches', *Journal for the History of Ideas*, XXVII,2, 1966, pp.245–64. There are two chapters on religion in J. Reulecke and W. Weber (eds.), *Fabrik, Familie, Feierabend: Beiträge zur Sozialgeschichte des Alltags im Industriezeitalter*, Wuppertal, 1978. *Social Compass*, XXVII, 2–3, 1980, is a special number on 'Religions of the Working Class', and includes articles on England, Spain and Germany in the nineteenth and twentieth centuries. There is a wealth of material on religion in F. Le Play, *Les ouvriers européens*, 6 vols., Tours, 1877; P. Göhre, *Three Months in a Workshop*, English translation, 1895; and C. Booth, *Life and Labour of the People in London*, 17 vols., 1902–3. One of the few episodes in more recent history to attract comparable interest in working-class religion was the worker-priest movement in France: see, for instance, G. Siefer, *The Church and Industrial Society*, English translation, 1964. My section on Wales depends mainly on E.T. Davies, *Religion in the Industrial Revolution in South Wales*, Cardiff, 1965, one of the few attempts to trace the development of working-class religion over a long period.

Chapter 8

There is a mass of data on contemporary religion in H. Mol (ed.), *Western Religion: A Country by Country sociological Inquiry*, The Hague, 1972; T. Beeson, *Discretion and Valour: Religious Conditions in Russia and Eastern Europe*, 1974; and *Acts of the 12th International Conference on the Sociology of Religion, The Hague, 1973: The contemporary Metamorphosis of Religion?* published by the Conférence Internationale de la Sociologie Religieuse, Lille, 1973. Among the interpreters of this evidence the most lucid is Bryan Wilson (e.g. *Contemporary Transformations of Religion*, 1976), the liveliest David Martin (e.g. *The Religious and the Secular*, 1969), the most original Thomas Luckmann (*The Invisible Religion*, English translation, New York, 1967). I have also drawn heavily on J.A. Coleman, *The Evolution of Dutch Catholicism, 1958–74*, Los Angeles, 1978. The more general studies tend to be stimulating but rather sweeping; the local studies are often stronger on facts than interpretation: there is a lack of substantial studies that attempt to test the general theories about the direction of contemporary religion against the realities of a particular situation. (However, since I completed this book, such a study has at last appeared: it is A.D. Gilbert, *The Making of Post-Christian Britain*, 1980.)

Appendix

Nominal religious affiliations of population in west-European countries in the 1960s.

Figures taken from H. Mol (ed.). *Western Religion*, The Hague, 1972, except for those on Great Britain, taken from D. Butler and D. Stokes, *Political Change in Great Britain*, Harmondsworth, 1971, p.160, and those for the Republic of Ireland taken from *Census of Population of Ireland*, 1961, VII, Dublin, 1965.

Austria	1961 census: Roman Catholic 89 per cent, Protestant 6 per cent, Other 1 per cent, None 4 per cent.
Belgium	No precise figures: about 96 per cent of population are baptised Roman Catholics.
Denmark	No precise figures: about 95 per cent of population are members of Lutheran church, and 4 per cent members of other churches.
France	In 1958 an estimated 92 per cent of children born were baptised Roman Catholics; about 2 per cent of the population Protestant, 1 per cent Jewish, 1 per cent Moslem.
Germany: East	1964 census: Protestant 59 per cent, Roman Catholic 8 per cent, Other 1 per cent, None 32 per cent.
West	1961 census: Protestant 51 per cent, Roman Catholic 44 per cent, Other 1 per cent, None or no answer 4 per cent.
Great Britain	1963 survey: Church of England 64 per cent, Church of Scotland or Presbyterian 9 per cent, Roman Catholic 9 per cent, free church 13 per cent, Jewish 1 per cent, Other 1 per cent, None 3 per cent.
	This survey showed 71 per cent claiming Church of England affiliation in England; the proportion claiming Church of Scotland affiliation must be around 75 per cent in Scotland; no separate figures have been published for Wales.
Ireland: North	1961 census: Roman Catholic 35 per cent, Presbyterian 29 per cent, Church of Ireland 24 per cent, Methodist 5 per cent, Other 7 per cent.
Republic	1961 census: Roman Catholic 95 per cent, Protestant 5 per cent, Other or no answer 1 per cent.
Netherlands	1960 census: Roman Catholic 40 per cent, Dutch Reformed

28 per cent, Gereformeerd 9 per cent, Other 4 per cent, None 18 per cent.

Norway	1960 census: Lutheran 96 per cent, Other 3 per cent, None 1 per cent.
Portugal	No precise figures: overwhelming majority Roman Catholic.
Spain	No precise figures: overwhelming majority Roman Catholic.
Sweden	State church records show 98 per cent of population affiliated in 1965, including some of those who also belong to other churches. About 4 per cent belonged to free churches.
Switzerland	1960 census: Protestant 53 per cent, Roman Catholic 46 per cent, Other 1 per cent, None 1 per cent.

Cities ■
Small towns or villages ○

PAS-
DE-
CALAIS
Tourcoing
Roubaix
Armentières
Lille
Arras ○
Amiens ■
Rouen ■
Compiègne
Reims ■
MARNE ARGONNE
LORRAINE
Bayeux
NORMANDY
Paris ■
Châlons-
sur- Marne
Ris-Orangis ○
BEAUCE
ALSACE
Brest ■
LÉON
BRITTANY
MORBIHAN
Rennes ■
Lorient ■
Vannes ■
Orleans ■
LOIRE VALLEY
LES
MAUGES
MAINE-
ET-
LOIRE
Saumur ○
NIÈVRE
VENDÉE
Mazières-en-Gâtine ○
SAÔNE -ET-LOIRE
La Rochelle ○
HAUTE-
VIENNE
LIMOUSIN
PUY-DE-DÔME
Clermont-
Ferrand ■
Lyon ■
ISÈRE
Grenoble ■
ALPS
Bordeaux ■
MASSIF
CENTRAL
Rodez ○
LANGUEDOC
CÉVENNES
PROVENCE
Nîmes ■
VAR
Toulouse ■
Lodève ○
Montpellier ○
St. Chinian
Lourdes ○
Marseille ■
PYRENEES

Index

More OPUS books

What is Theology?

Maurice Wiles

'Professor Wiles's book makes a first-rate introduction to the
subject. It has the honesty, the quiet persuasiveness and the
penetration which we have come to associate with his work. Let
those who undervalue theology read it and then ask themselves if
theology is either a soft option or an irrelevant pastime.'
Times Literary Supplement

'It is a lively, stimulating, and surprisingly thorough treatment, and
one which certainly conveyed to me 'the worthwhileness and the
excitement of the subject', which is indeed one of the author's
aims.' *Theology*

The Voice of the Past
Oral History

Paul Thompson

'Oral history gives history back to the people in their own words. And in giving a past, it also helps them towards a future of their own making . . . It thrusts life into history itself and it widens its scope. It allows heroes not just from the leaders, but from the unknown majority of the people.'

Paul Thompson argues that oral history can help to create a truer picture of the past, documenting the lives and feelings of all kinds of people, and that its value has been badly neglected by conventional historians. It can juxtapose professional opinion with interpretations of events drawn from all classes of society. In addition, the effect of collecting oral evidence can be to bind together communities, promote contact between generations, and give people a sense of roots in their own historical past.

'a pioneering and valuable book' *New Society*

Ethics since 1900

Mary Warnock

'In this lively and fascinating book Mrs Warnock tells with admirable clarity the story of the development of English moral philosophy in the twentieth century . . . most attractively written, spontaneous, forthright and unfuzzy.'
Times Literary Supplement

'The book is a classic among handbooks: unpretentious, but very individual, with a vigour and clarity which make it as attractive to read as it is instructive.' *Christian World*

Moral Philosophy

D. D. Raphael

Do moral philosophers have anything to say that is useful, let alone comprehensible, to the majority of us who have more down-to-earth concerns? An emphatic 'yes' is the reply given by Professor Raphael in this new book, whose purpose is to introduce moral philosophy to those with little or no acquaintance with the subject. In it he explains and discusses various doctrines such as utilitarianism, naturalism, and rationalism, stressing that far from being a purely esoteric subject, moral philosophy can and does have a bearing on practical problems experienced by those concerned with government, law, and social service. No one who reads this book is likely to make the mistake of thinking moral philosophy irrelevant.

Modern Spain

Raymond Carr

Taking as its starting-point the 'September Revolution' of 1868, *Modern Spain* looks at that country's troubled history over the last century. Professor Carr argues that much of modern Spanish history is explained by the tensions caused by imposing advanced liberal ideas and institutions on a conservative society. The various political regimes failed to win the allegiance of the masses, and the sudden political mobilization of the Second Republic of 1931 brought to the surface conflicts which previous regimes had buried and which the Republic itself could not master.

This important book synthesizes twenty years' work, incorporating much new research, and includes an examination of the present democratic regime and the problems it faces.

'This volume will be widely welcomed. He compresses with great skill and judgement in less than two hundred pages a comprehensive survey of the last hundred years giving particular attention to the period 1875–1930.' *Contemporary Review*

Change in British Society

A. H. Halsey

Most of us claim that we believe in liberty, equality, and fraternity –
but is it possible to achieve them without creating anarchy? Can
democracy survive increasing bureaucratic control over our lives? Is
Britain doomed to progressive economic and political decline?
Distinguished sociologist A. H. Halsey attempted to answer these
vital questions in a series of six Reith Lectures given in 1978. The
subject of much discussion and debate, they explored the ways in
which British society has changed since the beginning of the
century, and proposed solutions to major problems that are at once
sane and radical. The revised edition of this important book
includes a postscript by the author on developments during the last
two years.

This book is an Open University set text.